"Our creative li   anging—rather than
one stationary,   . For years I thought
creativity was limited to those onstage or at an easel, but a new day
has dawned. *Life Creative* has painted an all-inclusive picture, inviting
everyone to embrace their part in this present Renaissance."
       —**Sarah Bragg**, podcaster at SurvivingSarah.com

"Wendy and Kelli have told a beautiful and life-giving story, by telling the stories of many women—just like us—desiring to live the life
creative and steward what they've been given. This book will make you
aggressively grateful for the generation of women you've been born
into, and it will read like a breath of fresh air, a reminder to run in the
creative giftings you've been given."
       —**Jess Connolly**, author and speaker

"Kelli and Wendy understand that, yes, being a mom is about raising your children. But it's also about fully being the woman God created you to be and expressing His love like only you can. Their words
will support, encourage, and cheer you on in the art and adventure of
mothering."
       —**Holley Gerth**, *Wall Street Journal* best-selling author of
       You're Already Amazing

"Mothers carry deep within them an innate desire to create beauty
around them—whether it's   . In *Life
Creative*, Wendy and Kelli c   ide us all
with their wisdom and insi   ies while
also caring for the artist wit   r creative
moms."

D1280120

       —**Denise J. Hughes**, author of *Word Writers* and *On Becoming
       a Writer*, editorial coordinator for (in)courage, and
       founder of Deeper Waters Ministry

"This is a message that wondering, hungering, hurting, hoping hearts
need!"
       —**Becky Keife**, blogger, speaker, and mom, BeckyKeife.com

"I never expected this life. When I stepped out of the workplace to minister to my boys at home, I didn't know God would also call me to minister to mothers of boys all over the world. For years, I've struggled through these joint callings, simultaneously sure and unsure of myself in both. But I am sure of God, the Master Creative, who doesn't make mistakes as He asks us to use our gifts for His glory. Is there any way to be a mom *and* be obedient to my creative calling? I believe there is, and I look to moms like Kelli and Wendy to inspire me as I figure it out. If you're a mom struggling through multiple callings, read this book."

—**Brooke McGlothlin**, cocreator of The MOB Society and author of *Praying for Boys: Asking God for the Things They Need Most*

"The very first thing we learn about God in His word is that He 'created the heavens and the earth' (Gen. 1:1). We have a magnificently creative God who chose to make the pinnacle of His creation, humankind, in His image. Surely part of our image-bearing likeness to God is our ability to imagine and to create. Yet our creativity is sometimes lost in the busyness of life and mothering. In *Life Creative*, Wendy and Kelli offer fresh words of encouragement for moms to find natural, creative outlets right where they are—whether it is in a kitchen, on a canvas, through a lens, on a keyboard, or through some other medium. Wendy and Kelli's collection of stories about real-life creative moms is particularly inspiring and has led me to thoughtfully consider how I can best reflect the image of God through my own creative interests, as well as how I can model for my children the creative life that I desire for them to pursue as they mature."

—**Angie Mosteller**, author of *Christmas: Celebrating the Christian History of Classic Symbols, Songs and Stories*, celebratingholidays.com

"In a culture laden with 'mommy guilt,' *Life Creative* is a must-read for every mother who wants to hone her God-given creative gifts while encouraging her children to do the same. After feeling torn between mothering my three small children and pursuing my passion for writing during the first six years of motherhood, I finally came to peace with God giving me desires and gifts to bring Him glory. Motherhood and the creative life need not be at odds with each other! Wendy and Kelli's book will help readers realize this from the get-go. New and seasoned mothers alike need to read this book."

—**Erin Odom**, creator of thehumbledhomemaker.com and author of *More Than Just Making It*

"I am breathless. These are the things I believe but didn't have words to articulate . . . things that my soul knows are truth. I'm going back to read it all again, slowly."

—**Mindy Rogers**, teacher, writer, mom

"Never has there been a time like this for creative and artistic women to embrace the high calling of motherhood *and* the unique giftings God has given to each of us. There is indeed a movement—a Renaissance—of the creative woman, the creative mom. I'm grateful that Wendy and Kelli have chosen to encourage this generation of women, right now, to embrace their God-given creativity and steward it to the glory of God. This book is right on time."

—**Ruth Simons**, artist and writer, GraceLaced.com

"As a mom of two wild boys and a new baby girl, I am thankful for authentic moms like Wendy and Kelli who welcome women into this creative world in a manner that breaks down all barriers of comparison and the idea of measuring up."

—**Amber Tysl**, photographer and blogger

"As the mom of three kids, I need the wisdom of other moms, but most of all I need their companionship and gentle nod of understanding. Wendy and Kelli have offered that in the pages of this book in the most precious of ways: They've taken our hands, looked us in the eyes, and given us a gentle nod to help us move forward. *Life Creative* lets me be myself and find my best mothering there. Kudos, ladies. This book is a big exhale, a dear friend, and a powerful teacher."

—**Lisa Whittle**, speaker, author of *{w}hole* and *I Want God*

"*Life Creative* extends a hand across the lonely miles of motherhood to every woman who feels like she's lost herself in a sea of diapers and dishes. It breathes beauty and life and purpose into the everyday servanthood of mothering and reminds us that it's up to us to seize those very ordinary moments and turn them into something beautiful. I have never read anything like this, and as both a mother and an artist, I endorse it fully. The world needs *Life Creative*."

> —**Emily T. Wierenga**, author of five books including the
> memoir *Atlas Girl*

"Few things are as disorienting as the feeling that you have lost yourself in the midst of your own life. When demands of performing as a wife, mother, daughter, sister, friend, chef, medical aid, teacher, disciplinarian, theologian, artist, and more all pile up in even one day, it can seem nearly impossible to extract a true self from the many roles demanding your attention. A true Renaissance woman isn't torn in a million directions but is instead able to recognize the creative ways that God works in and through the various channels of her life. In motherhood and in ministry, Wendy and Kelli are women who have felt the tension and found the beauty of God's creativity through the changing seasons. *Life Creative* isn't simply an inspiration to embrace the seasons but a manual to continuously celebrate the creativity of God at work in you."

> —**Logan Wolfram**, speaker and author of *Curious Faith:*
> *Rediscovering Hope in the God of Possibility*

Life Creative

Inspiration for Today's Renaissance Mom

WENDY SPEAKE & KELLI STUART

Kregel
Publications

ISBN 978-0-8254-4410-4

Printed in the United States of America
16 17 18 19 20 21 22 23 24 25 / 5 4 3 2 1

We dedicate this book to the Master Creative,
the maker of heaven and earth,
the One who wove us then wooed us,
who stitched then saved our souls.
This is our *Surrendered Yes*.

CONTENTS

INTRODUCTION

A wise woman once said to me that there are only two lasting bequests we can hope to give our children. One of these is roots, the other, wings.

Hodding Carter Jr., American Journalist

It is the high calling of motherhood to raise our children in the grounded, unspoken knowledge that they belong and are safe within our hearts and homes. Roots grow deep in the supple soil of childhood. It is within the safety of the family that children begin to learn who they are. As they toddle at our sides, tentatively at first, we begin the joy-filled process of discovering their uniquely delightful God-design—who they were made to be, and how they were made to eventually soar off into the good works God prepared for each one of them. Their gifts are like hidden treasure that we unearth together.

What an honor it is to excavate these glorious gems from the lives of our little people, whispering into velvet ears, "God did such a good job when He made you. I love the way you build with Legos; I wonder what else you'll build with your hands when you're grown up. Maybe houses, or playgrounds for children." Murmuring our encouragement as we tuck them into bed, tickling soft skin.

Other times we shout it as they ascend the platform to receive that special award at school. "Most voracious reader!" we exclaim. "I wonder what God has planned for your life. Maybe one day you'll write stories for other children. Stories that are noble and good, and that inspire kids to do great things!"

A mother's love tills the fertile soil of her children's lives so that their roots might be healthy, all the while rooting them on to sprout wings and soar. Many books have already been written to encourage mothers on this very front. Books about the roots and wings our children need to thrive, because both extremities are required for a rich, fulfilling life. And yet sometimes in the process a mom's own wonderful design can get lost for a season. It's not unusual. Nor is it the end of the world, though sometimes it feels that way. We call it *sacrifice*. We call it *motherhood*.

Back at the beginning, when this book was just a dream, I told a crafty girlfriend with three preschool-aged children about our plans to encourage creative moms. As I finished describing the basic premise, my tenderhearted, creative friend grabbed my hand and thanked me. I was surprised to see tears pool in her eyes. "No one's ever spoken to that part of me before," she whispered.

> A mother's natural bent toward creativity doesn't just wither and die with the birth of a child. This core component remains part of her intricate design.

She went on to tell me about the day she announced her second pregnancy to a group of close friends. Upon hearing her delightful news, one of them quipped, "It's time to put away your sewing machine. You won't be doing that for a while." The natural assumption was that children would now supersede all other desires. Her time would be too consumed, after all, to even consider her own creative pursuits.

There's truth there, we all feel it, but it's also true that a mother's natural bent toward creativity doesn't just wither and die with the birth of a child. This core component remains part of her intricate design.

Dear friends, I've got some good news to share: every mom was created creative. Each and every one of us has been endowed with the Creator's ability to imagine something out of nothing. We call this inspiration, and isn't that how the universe came to be? His creation first imagined and then executed. From nothing He made every atom, every molecule. And we were fashioned to live, move, and breathe in the fullness of His creative likeness!

Here in this present season, however, our creativity may look different than before. Some inventive moms create meals for their toddlers where veggies are ingeniously blended into sauces and muffins, while others are able to grow their creative passions into successful home businesses. Many cautiously fit their interests into everyday life like a private hobby, scrapbooking their way through their children's growing-up years. The more roots-centric moms find joy in creating gorgeous parties for the benefit of close family and friends, while others long constantly to spread their wings and fly on the wind of inspiration.

And so this book is for all moms: those who consider themselves artistic and those who suddenly and surprisingly find themselves inspired in the midst of these mothering years. All are invited to celebrate and explore this *life creative*.

We are two women writing this missive of encouragement as one voice, because we want to honor your life at home and your dreams beyond and the myriad places between, and one woman rarely has the vantage point to examine it all. In fact, each chapter tells the stories of many others living creatively within this blessed season of motherhood. Together we, *I*, endeavor to paint one cohesive yet diverse portrait of faith, family, and the breadth and width of a woman's creative dreams.

> God has prepared for Himself one great song of praise throughout eternity, and those who enter the community of God join in this song. It is the song that the "morning stars sang together and all the sons of God shouted for joy" at the creation of the world (Job 38:7).
>
> Dietrich Bonhoeffer

I don't know if it takes a village to raise a child, but I do believe it requires a whole lot of women to raise up a mom. Picture the book you hold in your hands as an intersection where the snuffed-out fire of uniquely creative you crosses paths with an entire community of artists passionately pursuing this life in Christ. Each one gifted in various forms, but all united by our common season of active motherhood. I'm telling their stories—*your* stories—and encouraging all moms, no matter the circumstances or season, to discover again the joy of chasing their dreams, while also remaining deeply rooted at home.

This is for them, and it's for you—uniquely designed, creative *you*.

> I don't know if it takes a village to raise a child, but I do believe it requires a whole lot of women to raise up a mom.

Chapter One

A New Renaissance

People are moved to wonder by mountain peaks,
by vast waves of the sea, by broad waterfalls on
rivers, by the all-embracing extent of the ocean,
by the revolutions of the stars. But in themselves
they are uninterested.

Augustine, AD 399

I see you there awkwardly turning your wrist, trying to conceal the fact that you're uploading another artfully edited picture of your children to Instagram. Does your husband laugh, and do you blush? Have you convinced yourself that what you're doing is silly? Or are you halfway holding on to hope that each picture is an offering of something beautiful and worthy and encouraging? *Because it is.* And so are you.

You are an offering altogether beautiful, worthy, and wonderful. You, dear Mom, are the poster child of a brand new Renaissance! This movement is not coursing across Europe as it did in the 1500s, or blaring from the jazz clubs of Harlem, pumping out into the humid New York skyline of the 1920s. It is, instead, flowing out of homes, nurseries, kitchens, and living rooms around the world through cyberspace, uploaded and shared with friends and public circles, allowing this generation of Renaissance women to move faster than Michelangelo or Langston Hughes ever dreamed.

Here's the most amazing part: you're just being you—altogether beautiful you, amidst the chaotic rhythms of motherhood. Capturing great glimpses of glory with your camera at the sandlot over brown bag lunches. And when you lay your little ones down for naps, out it flows—the inspired offering of a creative woman.

I'm here to tell you this is a worthy use of your life: both the grand offering of motherhood, and the smaller gifting of artistic self-expression. I hear you and see you, and am experiencing you as you pin your way through new recipes and craft ideas. As you redesign your child's room and paint her walls with murals, I stand in awe of your outpouring. This is the flow of a Renaissance mom.

Of course, it's not easy, is it? This glorious Renaissance most often happens in the quiet moments, many of them hidden in the dark of night after children are asleep, or early mornings before tiny feet pitter-patter to your side. You're sneaking it in, because life dictates that you do so. But I see you as you work.

I see the artistry eeking out of those slivers of silent moments . . . stolen, sequestered, and sanctified. I've taken the time to consider the way you work dough, the way you fly that needle through fabric, plan a birthday party with handcrafted banners, and type out the poetry of your days into short blog posts. And I invite you to join me in this observation, to consider the way you were created *creative*. I offer this invitation with a warning, though. It's not uncommon for women to experience shame and embarrassment when they pause to focus on themselves, particularly when they are in the thick of this others-centered season. This book is a safe place where we seek out together what God might have intended when, just days after He hung the heavens and fixed the Earth in place, He fashioned us in His image—creative.

Some of you are stay-at-home moms, each day carving out those rare moments that you get to call your own. This book is for you, a love letter to your creative heart. Others of you are on-the-job moms, fitting your creativity into the packed places of work-life balance. Either way, consider me your cheerleader, shaking my pom-poms and shouting 2-4-6-8, because I appreciate you! And so do your children as you decorate their lives and keepsake their memories. Your husband, coworkers, and friends are grateful for the gift of your creativity and the marvelous meals served on the tablecloth of your hospitality.

You are the face of a brand-new Renaissance. Look in the mirror and take a deep breath, knowing you have been affirmed.

But let us also acknowledge that it's a dance, this creative life in the midst of mothering—a dance that threatens our balance. You understand balance as you hang your canvas upon the wall. You choose balance as you create a website to market your treasures, and balance again as you purposefully shut down your computer when it's time to join your family around the table. And in all the understanding and the choosing, you may just find that there is no such thing as balance after all. Some days it's all mothering, and other days you're lopsided the other way. Like dancing on a tightrope as it sways in the wind, one foot in front of the other, each creative step and mothering step, back and forth.

So read on, dear Renaissance Moms, not just to receive affirmation, but also to find encouragement and help in this dance between family, faith, and flourishing creativity.

Renaissance man (*noun*). A cultured man who is knowledgeable, educated, interested, and/or proficient in a wide range of subjects.

A Renaissance man or woman, or *mom* as the case may be, is a term reserved for one who is generally known to be talented in many different areas. "She bakes, she sews, she sings . . . what a Renaissance woman!" Though most Renaissance men of the late Middle Ages were artistically gifted, the term was not relegated to the arts alone, but rather included a wide skill set. Leonardo DaVinci, for example, was a master painter and sculptor, but also studied the stars and charted the anatomy of man. DaVinci was both artist and scientist, a man who could seemingly do it all. And so can we, perhaps, but not all at once. And not all today.

During our college days, Jules smelled of citrus and cinnamon when everyone else smelled of Dr. Pepper and granola. She was altogether different and intriguing because she dared live off campus and make her own meals rather than join us in the cafeteria.

Jules was a poet, an actress, a dancer, and, I thought at the time, quite possibly a fairy.

She no longer performs onstage, but this doesn't mean her creative life has been lost. It's morphed out of the theater and into the home instead. Yet through the passage of time, one thing remains consistent—she still smells of exotic spices. These days, however, instead of keeping to herself in a small off-campus bungalow, Jules has swung open the doors of her family home in Los Angeles, feeding women from her kitchen with healthy meals and rich conversation. Her passion to blend art and life within her own four walls over a wooden cutting board has overflowed into lives the world over.

Knee deep in mothering, Jules creatively inspires women not only to feed their families healthy, beautiful meals but to nourish their own souls as well. Encouraging weary moms who have lost their passion for the kitchen to rediscover the joy, the art, and the honor of filling little bellies and hearts alike. Jules models this joy with recipes that read more like a conversation over a platter of persimmons, figs, and all sorts of vegetables straight from the earth. Blogging her way through farmers' markets as her children pull their wagon behind her, it's all swathed together into one inspiring picture of a Renaissance mom.

It was another Jules who helped coin the phrase *Renaissance* in literature. Jules Michelet's *Histoire de France*, in 1855, was one of the first to fashion a label upon the miracle of creativity that pushed through Europe from the fourteenth through seventeenth centuries. Art was being born again after the dark ages of European history.

The Dark Ages

Renaissance literally translates "rebirth." How appropriate, and how inspiring for mothers of young children, because there are indeed dark ages in our mothering as well. Dark years when long nights and overwhelming days roll ceaselessly together, and hormones swing out. Then suddenly our tears are tempered by the glory moments of beauty. Soft morning cuddles. Childlike faith taking root. The handprint art we frame, and the birthday dress that magically turns her into a real-life princess.

In these dark ages, amidst the unending flow of meeting everyone's needs, the arts seem to get lost for a season, as they did in the darkest chapters of world history. But here's an amazing truth about the literal Dark Ages and the Renaissance that followed: it was the church that protected much of the ancient writings when the world went black. It was the church that tucked them away alongside relics and artifacts. As though God Himself were holding the arts there in the dark. And when it was time for our world's creative rebirth, much of it flowed from the church.

Now implant that in your own heart on a personal level. In your darkest mothering days, when the hours stretch long and weary, and your time and energy leak out upon the never-ending list of chores, God Himself is holding on to those creative and seemingly lost parts of you. And when He Himself calls you to new life on the other side of this overwhelming season, He will give it all back—along with so much more.

If I say, "Surely the darkness will overwhelm me,
And the light around me will be night,"
Even the darkness is not dark to You,
And the night is as bright as the day.
Darkness and light are alike to You. (Ps. 139:11–12)

Our darkest days are as light to Him. He sees us all illuminated, from beginning to end. He knows all, is over all, purposing each dark day to radically juxtapose the glory of the Renaissance to come. For God is the master of rebirth, reigning sovereign over the dark ages of our personal history. Yes, God is the author of this Renaissance!

I understand all of this well, the death and dying sensation of servitude. Even back when I prepared to say "I do," a small part of me cried out "I don't," because I could foresee the natural flow away from me and into them on the other side of marriage and children.

There we were in the pastor's office, young, naïve, and love-struck, counseling our way through the engagement as we planned the wedding. Thankfully, the pastor didn't just want a well-planned wedding for us. He saw ahead into our marriage and somehow perceived my fears, so he turned to me and asked, "What are you most afraid of?" I sputtered, stuttered, and stopped.

He let me think in the awkward quiet, and it grew hot as my future husband waited for an answer. Finally, "I'm afraid of losing myself" came from somewhere deeper than my conscious mind—a prophetic deep. And our counselor nodded and smiled, and waited for me to continue.

"Not right away, maybe, but over the years. Because I love this man, and want to pour myself out for him and into him; and one day I want to stay at home with our children, and pour myself out for them . . . but what if I get all poured out and lose the stuff that makes me special? I don't even know what it might look like. But what if I do?"

He nodded again then shifted his gaze to my fiancé, to the one who had not yet done any wrong in my eyes. The older said to the younger, "Do you hear what she's saying? She's going to lay her life down to lift you up. But this is only going to work if you do the same for her." It was intense, with my man nodding emphatically like he understood, but neither of us really did because we hadn't lived it yet.

Now here we are fifteen years in, and while he's tried to lift me up and serve me back, it's not a simple equation where y = x, because his y chromosome doesn't always equal my x. So here I am, giving myself away for all these people that I'm head over heels in love with, and he's off working, laying his life down for us in a whole other sense, and all that good counseling has to find its way to application. So we try to figure it out late at night, once the children are in bed, and we meet up together in the dark.

But when he falls asleep, I'm still awake, and I see that my premarried fears were rooted in something real and common among women. Perhaps you also see yourself struggling in this lonely place, having laid it all down for the loved ones in your midst. Perhaps you too know these dark ages of mothering, where passion for life, ministry, and art seem lost.

If that's where you are, dear Mom, I urge you not to mourn the loss for more than a moment. This is not the end of who you are. As you pour yourself out to your beloveds, day after day, longing for time to create but not knowing where the moments will magically appear, I urge you to cling to the picture of Him holding your art with the same tenderness that He holds your eternal soul. Caressing each moment protectively in His palm, guarding it as you sacrificially give of yourself.

These dark ages are not the end of who He created you to be. They're the night before the dawn, the winter before spring, the labor before new life. Like the flip side of an Ecclesiastes coin, a time to plant and a time to reap, a time to rend and a time to mend; a time to pour into young souls, cultivating their roots, and a time to send them out with their own strong wings; a time to know death but also a time to know rebirth. Renaissance. This is our anthem song as we march through the dark: a time to lay our lives down, but also a time to be lifted up again. Look up expectantly—this is only the beginning!

> There is an appointed time for everything. And there is a time for every event under heaven. (Eccl. 3:1)

His plans are for seasons and each season requires new plans. When our children are very young we inevitably find ourselves in a season of sacrifice. This sacrifice will look different for each of us. Some will sacrifice artistic careers to stay home with the children, filling the days with fantastic adventures, hectic trips to the grocery store, and more laundry than can possibly be tallied. Others may have to sacrifice time in the home *along with* creative expression in order to help make ends meet financially, dropping children off at day care, praying through traffic, wishing it were easier.

Make no mistake about it—sacrifice is never easy. I say this not as someone far removed from sacrificial loving but as someone presently living deep in the trenches. The monitor by my side hums with the white noise of a fan as I type this message out, reminding me of the newborn who's swaddled like an inchworm one room over. I know I should sleep myself, sinking into a few hours of slumber before her cries draw me to her side again. But this message calls, and so I sacrifice the sleep. Yes, I understand the hollow places of sacrifice, and I agree. It is difficult.

His plans are for seasons and each season requires new plans.

But then, if it weren't difficult, it wouldn't be a sacrifice.

Perhaps you're in the midst of a similarly constraining season of sacrifice. But these early mothering days do not define the length and width of your forever life. It is true that He made you a wife and a mother, but your timeline holds more from cradle to graduation to grave. More seasons and more facets to the jewel we call your abundant life. And part of your *more* is the fact that He created you creative.

Because of that masterful design, you ache today to live in the fullness of your nature: to sing or to write, to paint, to decorate, to sew, to build, or to bake. You have ideas, some of which keep you awake at night. You feel them calling and long to answer, but you're not sure how. You roll over to find your husband sleeping soundly in the dark, and perhaps feel a bit resentful. He knows his purpose; you wish that you could embrace your mission with the same gutsy pride.

> This Renaissance is the breeze to give you flight, but it all starts with the One who gave you wings.

Here's the charge: I believe you can. Though some days (or seasons) it's an awkward, bumpy ride, the creative in you is still there, in the dark perhaps, waiting for that coming time when you'll once again stretch your creative wings, and—yes, my friend—you just may fly.

> There is freedom waiting for you,
> On the breezes of the sky,
> And you ask, "What if I fall?"
> Oh but my darling,
> What if you fly?
> Erin Hanson

This Renaissance is the breeze to give you flight, but it all starts with the One who gave you wings. Rest fully in the knowledge that your creativity was not an accident, nor is your present circumstance of motherhood. They are both gifts from Him, both parts of a Master plan, woven and knit into beautiful you. God has a plan for your creativity, even in the seemingly dormant years—the dark ages before the dawning light.

When I think back to that day in our pastor's office, I'm moved by my prophetic fears. However, I believe that our counselor, though well intentioned, didn't get it quite right. While he encouraged my husband to support me, I've found that I can't depend on him to fill me and hold me up all the time. I need more—something more, *Someone* more.

During the hardest and darkest seasons of sacrifice, the only one able to lift us *fully* from the dark and give us renewed vision for life is our Savior. His Spirit and His life and His power holding us up as we lay it all down.

> He put a new song in my mouth, a song of praise to our God;
> Many will see and fear
> And will trust in the LORD. (Ps. 40:3)

So you singers reading now, this figurative new song of praise is coming your way—and maybe a literal one too. For the visual artists and the wordsmiths, the seamstresses and cooks, and you decorators in our midst, a new song is prepared for you as well. Each melody tailored to your specific gift, to fit your life, your loved ones, and your expanding dreams. And no matter how it flows, selling your jewelry or painting canvases, designing websites or taking family portraits, or out to the world through the tender vibrato of your shaking voice, God has a purpose for each note!

This Renaissance song is kingdom work.

For many years as a young mother, I clung to the light of John 15:13, chiseling my own translation into each new day: "Greater love has *no mom* than this, that she lay down her life for her family." I clung to these words during days when I longed for more but could not find the time or energy to fit anything else in. In the midst of it all, I felt great shame for my lack of contentment. I pushed on sacrificially, offering this mantra up to the Lord each morning as I placed my bare feet square on the ground of the new day.

Then one morning as my toes touched the cool wood floor and my mothering verse rolled off my tongue, I felt a pause in my soul. After many long years of persevering in sacrificial love, God's whisper came softly but firmly, "Yes, it's true I'm calling you to sacrifice, but I don't actually want you to die." It was then I saw myself walking around our home as a ghost of the woman God created me to be. His sweet words displaced my premature death, breathing new life into my heart and my home, resurrecting long-buried parts.

> Could it be that God's will for us isn't that we lay down our passions and our lives on the altar to be burned, but that we lay them instead at the feet of our Savior to be used? A living sacrifice.

My goal now is to breathe this whisper into your heart: to inspire you in the chapters ahead to anticipate His lifting hands, to embrace this rebirth, this *Renaissance*, by embracing fearfully and wonderfully made, creative you.

Do you see now, dear sister, that He doesn't actually want you to die in these mothering years? He was so purposeful in our creative design! This is you and me, and a whole army of moms, gathering around these pages, redefining what a laid-down woman looks like. Could it be that God's will for us isn't that we lay down our passions and our lives on the altar to be burned, but that we lay them instead at the feet of our Savior to be used? A living sacrifice.

In His time. For His glory.

Wonderfully Made

They came out of the pool a tangle of wet limbs. Wet suits were thrown over the backs of chairs, and I lifted the youngest up into a warm, sun-drenched towel, hugging him briefly until he squirmed from my grasp and followed the others into the house.

Sweet, quiet moments of solitude are starting to come more frequently as the children grow up and into their independence. And as they transition, I do too, which is why one of my present goals is to sit down and simply be still at least once a day. Not folding clothes, or even reading stories aloud to my kiddos on the couch, but the *ceasing from striving* sort of stillness that takes discipline. And so I sat back down and breathed in deeply the dry earth smells around our home.

It took only a moment for me to hear birds chirping various melodies; so many different types, each singing its joyful hymn from the branches above my head. And the songs floated up, unhindered and free. Layered into the sound track of creation was the rustling of dried leaves as lizards darted in the foliage nearby. A barely audible tinkling played from the eucalyptus branches beside the house. Two dogs barked, a horse whinnied, and the sound of my children's laughter floated out from the sliding glass door still slightly ajar.

What a glorious song, this life that surrounds me, teeming with creativity all its own. Back before children, I often stood in awe of God's creative handiwork throughout nature. Everything seemed to testify to *Elohim*, Creator God.

> The heavens are telling of the glory of God;
> And their expanse is declaring the work of His hands. (Ps. 19:1)

Then when my children were born, my understanding of God as creator was taken to a whole new level. How purposefully He wove each one together with their personalities and skin tones and eye colors and the varying pitches in their laughter!

> For You formed my inward parts;
> You wove me in my mother's womb.
> I will give thanks to You, for I am fearfully and wonderfully made;
> Wonderful are Your works,
> And my soul knows it very well. (Ps. 139:13–14)

I can't help but praise Him for His handiwork on display in their little lives. And since each miracle birth I have watched eagerly and expectantly, believing every day of their precious lives was planned before one of them came to be. And yet, only since the miracle *rebirth* of my own life have I been able to see that these psalms were written also about me. God created *me*. He knit *me* together in my mother's womb. All His works are wonderful, I know that full well, but only recently have I embraced the fact that *I* am one of His wonderful works.

And so are you.

Chapter Two

Confined Yet Unhindered

> When our dreams remain unfulfilled or unattended we begin to experience life as a nightmare. Our dreams are intended to serve as the material from which we create. When we do not create we live beneath our intention. When we live without intention we drift and lose ourselves. Humans must create—not only to express ourselves but to find ourselves.
>
> Erwin Raphael McManus

I sat next to Sally Clarkson at a small homeschool convention in the fall of 2010. Her book, *The Mission of Motherhood*, was—and remains—my favorite book on mothering, so sitting next to this feminine giant thrilled me to the core. In the minutes before she took the podium, we shared tea and conversation. She asked me about myself, and I told her of my dreams to creatively minister to women beyond the confines of our home. When I revealed the ages of my children, two, four, and six at the time, she reached out her hand and clasped mine.

"Make sure your children are taken care of before you step beyond your home for ministry. Home is where everything starts when they are this young. Home is where everything starts."

Though her words were meant to encourage, my heart winced. I fought the tears that stung my eyes, and forced a smile. At the time I was still reeling in the dark ages of my personal confinement, trying to remember the fullness of life before children. Though I loved our baby powder–scented days, I ached for self-expression. That's why I shared something about myself unrelated to my role as mother. I was gasping for air in the years that preceded the Renaissance, and I felt reprimanded for dreaming.

"Home is where everything starts."
—Sally Clarkson

But now I stand on the other side of those crazy early years, and my encouragement to other creative mothers echoes Sally's. Looking back, I see what she was saying, summed up in those last words: *Home is where everything starts.*

The following Sunday morning, I sat close to my husband in the sanctuary pew. All our children were miraculously healthy and in their Sunday school classes, so my hands and heart were free to grab hold of the morning's worship. The instant the music began, tears started rolling heavy and hot down my weary face. A woman across the aisle, twenty years my senior, got up to bring me a pouch of tissues and nodded, like she understood. I was at the end of my own strength.

The pastor ascended all three stairs in one great leap as the musicians left the platform. I blew my nose, wiped my eyes, and leaned forward in great anticipation. Without his usual humor, the preacher simply asked us to open our Bibles to the very end of the book of Acts. We'd been working our way through Paul's account of the early church for months, and had come to the end. So much like me.

I found my way to Acts 28 as the sound of pages turning in God's Living Word rustled through the lofty sanctuary. Though the preacher

began reading at the beginning of the chapter, my eye caught hold of
verses 30–31, and I heard God's faithful whisper calling me back to life
once again.

> He stayed two full years . . . and was welcoming all who came
> to him, preaching the kingdom of God and teaching concern-
> ing the Lord Jesus Christ with all openness, unhindered.

As I mulled over these verses, I remembered that the apostle Paul
was writing to us from prison. He was under house arrest. Confined to
home, unable to leave. As I read it again and again, my gospel-loving,
artistic heart that used to dream of going out and touching the world
got all constrained in my chest. I was just barely making it through our
day-to-day life. Though I used to hunger for ministry and creativity and
inspiring the world, these days I simply longed for bedtime. Some of
you are nodding your heads because you know. *You're there now.*

> **confined** (*adjective*). Imprisoned. Forced to stay within limits
> and prevented from venturing beyond certain boundaries.

Confined. The word stuck like a thorn in my flesh, because sometimes this mothering gig feels like a prison. We're under house arrest.
Though we love our blessed captors, there are long days and weeks and
years no one ever prepared us for. This confinement can be quite literal
for the stay-at-home mom, as she fights to leave home for the most basic
of errands. For the working mom, the confinement may be situational,
as she wars between a longing to be at home and the desire, or the
necessity, to head out again.

No matter your reality, whether you're home every day or working in
an office, your heart is chained to the small people that captured you.
And they *have* captured you, haven't they? Captured your heart in the
most magnificent ways. But they've also locked you up like Paul. And
there you sit, waiting and yearning for the day you can break free from
your chains and start living your own dreams again. Of course the

guilt-laced irony is that you most likely dreamed long and hard about having a family. I know I did! And I'm not saying that I don't want them. I simply want me, too.

It's messy and terribly confusing, this confinement—messier than the diapers and the constant roll of snacks in need of sweeping up. It's messier than play dough dried on the kitchen table and sand from the park ground into the crevices of the wood floor. It's messier than the tearful good-byes in the mornings, or the rushed dinners at night before bed. The mess supersedes the physical and grinds its way emotionally and spiritually into our very beings.

We're left worn out and unbalanced from the emotional mess of house arrest. Depression threatens as we surrender so much of ourselves to the high calling of motherhood. And a spiritual mess develops if we forget to abide, and instead cling to survive. My heart and mind conversed about all these things and more as the pastor preached his sermon that Sunday morning.

Soft light streamed in through stained glass windows, and I looked again at the verses resting patiently in my lap. "He stayed two full years . . . and was welcoming all who came to him, preaching the kingdom of God and teaching concerning the Lord Jesus Christ with all openness, unhindered." Suddenly the color-drenched sun danced its way into the sanctuary and lit up the description of the apostle Paul under house arrest. The fragmented pieces of light dissected and rearranged the words, allowing me to see new application and give me vision for this season at home.

> **unhindered** (*adjective*). Free. Not held back or prevented from action, movement, or progress.

Unhindered. The word coupled with *confined* and became for me the key that God used to open wide my prison doors. *Confined yet unhindered;* the thought began to shake my chains loose and scales dropped from my eyes. Though imprisoned, there was gospel power flowing through Paul, out of his home and into the world. And though we may be confined, the same power is present and purposed in our lives as well.

There in the church, trembling in the pew, I caught a vision of this gospel life without hindrance; the gospel that the grave could not contain; the gospel that my own circumstances could not confine. I gasped audibly, because I finally comprehended the miracle of a mother's ultimate purpose in the home, and the blessed fruit God intends us to cultivate there: fruit in the lives of our children, fruitful ministry to those we welcome around our table, and *eventually* fruit out into the world.

All while under house arrest.

Whether your present circumstances have you literally confined to your home in the day-to-day mundane moments of motherhood, or circumstantially confined as you strike the tenuous balance of a working mom, know that your confinement has purpose.

The Great Commission

You've read the words and heard the phrase, listened to countless pastors and wondered what part you play in the Great Commission. Could it be that the fact that we are an artistic bunch of confined ragamuffins has not escaped His eye or plan? That's the question this book hopes to answer. In fact, it is my most ardent belief that our generation of creative moms is finding and forging new roads out into the world from our very homes. Confined with our talents and our passion for Christ, a tidal wave is surging, ready to flood the world with creative expressions of faith.

> God always intended His Great Commission to start this way. Indeed there is a biblical pattern to our going out into the world, and this pattern most assuredly begins in our homes.

And you'll be delighted to discover that God always intended His Great Commission to start this way. Indeed there is a biblical pattern to our going out into the world, and this pattern most assuredly begins in our homes.

Consider the Great Commission and the verse that sends us out:

> Go therefore and make disciples of all the nations, baptizing them in the name of the Father and the Son and the Holy Spirit. (Matt. 28:19)

> But you will receive power when the Holy Spirit has come upon you; and you shall be My witnesses both in Jerusalem, and in all Judea and Samaria, and even to the remotest part of the earth. (Acts 1:8)

Christ's last words to His disciples on earth were to "make disciples of all the nations." But the account in Acts gives us a pattern, or an *order*, to our going out. Starting in Jerusalem, which was *home* for the early church, and in the same way for us is our literal *home*; then to Judea and Samaria, our neighborhoods and community, churches, schools, and mercy ministries; and then finally out into the world.

It Starts at Home

Home is where everything starts. These walls are home to the little hearts entrusted to our care. These children are the disciples we are to make and teach, first and foremost. Confined for a time here at home, God is showing us our starting line in this Great Commission race. Beginning in Jerusalem.

So we put our noses down and get to the great work for which we've been commissioned. We live grace, and we sing our gospel song, tucking them in and tickling their backs, not rushing the final pages of *Goodnight Moon* for the sake of a project half started in the other room. Because one of these days the sun will set and the moon will rise, and they won't ask to hear the story again. So we live it to the fullest extent we can today. Because there's unhindered gospel power in our undivided attention.

Can't you hear your children's testimony years from now? "Mama loved me with all she had, so I trusted the One she said loved me most.

Yeah, the Bible told me so too, but I sing it out, 'Yes, Jesus loves me, my *Mama* told me so.'"

And another wonderful step to this miracle waltz, Renaissance Moms, is that we pour our love out in all the fullness of who we are as creatives! Over a palette of watercolors, we pour out; at the table making tissue-paper stained-glass projects, we pour out; framing and hanging the acrostic poems our children help to create out of their names, we pour out; over the baking sheet of hot oatmeal cookies, we pour out; dreaming up words that become stories in their beds at night, we pour out; stringing beads and making necklaces out of Cheerios at the breakfast table, we pour out. All this poured out, sacrificial love, splashing over their little bodies and hearts in the years of our blessed confinement.

Make no mistake, it's not easy, and it's not always pretty. Because while a creative mom can decorate it and make it beautiful, the reality of training these little lives isn't always Pinterest perfect. As a matter of fact, it reminds me of potty training: messy and you can't go anywhere. This task takes all our attention, until suddenly we're done. They're potty trained! And we celebrate by *leaving the house* and going to the zoo without a diaper bag or stroller, because that baby is a big kid now!

No doubt many of you are still doing the intense work of training at home. Not necessarily potty training, but the seemingly endless work of heart training. Whether you're home all day, or your most dedicated hours of training are in the mornings and evenings, each day you wake up and recommit to your personal Jerusalem, pouring your entire ministry into the little ones in your arms, at your side. You're not looking yet to Samaria and Judea, though you dream of the literal and creative freedom to come, there on the other side of *Goodnight Moon*.

When my children were very young, we lived on a small cul-de-sac. Our little home sat at the top of a hill where, looking down, we could see our neighbors outside playing every afternoon. My children, fresh from their naps, would clamor for the door, ready to dash down the hill as fast as their little legs would carry them. Pulling out two old lawn chairs, my neighbor Carol invited me to sit in her driveway, on the cold days and the hot days. As our little ones played in the dirt around us, we were usually joined by more neighborhood friends, all of them ready for a little fresh air and interaction.

How those days ministered to me. Though we were only a few steps from our home, it was just enough to get me out and away, which alleviated the strain of confinement I felt. I needed those times with grownups as much as my kids needed to run off their toddler energy. It was so simple, this ministering to my heart. It required no more than a ratty lawn chair, some good conversation, and, every once in awhile, a Diet Coke from the garage refrigerator.

Carol welcomed all who came to her, and in her welcoming she ministered gospel love to weary souls. Not necessarily verbally—though Carol never shied away from speaking of her faith—but simply by the act of opening her driveway, lifting her garage door, and letting us all know we were welcome. Right there in her Jerusalem.

There are others, so much like my Carol, creatively encouraging women to this same end. Reaching out, embracing, and extending Christ's love from their dining room tables and cul-de-sac corners of the world. Women like Kristin Schell who was simply inspired by God's command to love her neighbors, completely unaware of the revival she would launch. And *revival* is the right word, though she didn't raise a tent. It was just an ordinary wooden picnic table purchased from Lowes and painted Sherwin Williams's Nifty Turquoise. She dragged this cheery table out onto the front lawn with the help of her husband and their four children, and placed it beneath the large magnolia tree at the end of the street. And that was all it took.

The very first day she set out her table, a neighbor Kristin had never met stopped by and sat down. Before long, many neighborhood friends, old and new, were dropping by to share the carafe of coffee she had brewed. From those early days, the doors of hospitality flew wide open, and one ordinary mom with a can of paint learned anew God's mission-minded plan for neighborhoods. Since then this turquoise revival has taken off, inspiring thousands of women across the country to live and preach the gospel message from their own front yards.

Paul didn't just *write* to early believers while under house arrest, biding his time until his release. He literally welcomed all who would come to him around his table. We can do the same. Though maybe all we can manage at this point is a case of Diet Coke waiting in the fridge out in the garage. Or maybe you're inspired to express your faith to family and friends in more tangible ways. Sending handcrafted neighborhood invites, taking pictures of the neighborhood fun and emailing them out to moms and dads just down the street. It *is* possible, in the fullness of this life season, to do what Paul and Kristin and Carol all challenge us to do—minister from our homes. When we reach out from our figurative prison cells, we have the power to arrest others right back!

> This is the Great Commission wearing its everyday clothes. Rolling up sleeves, pulling hair back into a messy bun, and opening the door to your Jerusalem.

> He stayed two full years . . . and was welcoming all who came to him, preaching the kingdom of God and teaching concerning the Lord Jesus Christ with all openness, unhindered. (Acts 28:30–31)

Just as your children read the gospel account of God's great love for them in your poured-out care, your guests experience it too. Everyone who comes to you is in desperate need, whether they know it or not, especially in this life stage. Even a believing mama needs to rest on her friend's lawn chair as the children play together. This is the Great Commission wearing its everyday clothes. Rolling up sleeves, pulling hair back into a messy bun, and opening the door to your Jerusalem.

Ministering creatively from confinement will look different for every woman. It will look different for the mother with young children than it does for the mother with older kids. It won't look the same for working moms as it does for those who stay at home. It will be different for the writer than it is for the crafter. This Great Commission call begins in each unique home and heart, each style of faith and family, flowing from our confinement out into the world.

Your life at home is where it all begins, not just in the great big, inspired moments but also in the small, simple, ordinary ones. So keep it up! Keep serving your blessed little captors, and keep ministering with creativity and faith to the ones who join you around your table and in your yard. Open wide your life creative, *and your life ordinary*. Open it up and pour it out and lay it down and give it away.

For mothers of young children, great creativity and the Great Commission both begin at home, finding their way up and out of the dark ages together.

Keep reading, my friends, because we're just getting started. There is an order to our going out, and Jerusalem is only the beginning.

Chapter Three

Beyond Jerusalem

I cannot rest, I must draw, however poor the result, and when I have a bad time come over me it is a stronger desire than ever.

Beatrix Potter, 1884

She closes her eyes at night and the colors dance. With a sigh, she gives herself over to the images, the pictures she longs to paint. There are canvases, waiting to be filled, stacked in the garage. Tubes of paint, sealed tight, in the basement. Untouched brushes splayed throughout the supply box.

She is a painter.

She not only sees images but somehow also manages to capture them. The swish of brushstroke against canvas, against paper, against a wall is like a symphony to her creative heart.

She is an artist.

She wakes to the sound of tiny feet running to her bed. Flopping down beside her, the little one begins his morning jabber before she can coherently formulate a response. The night was too short. There was a baby to feed and scary dreams to chase away.

She is a mother.

She tries to conjure up the images that danced vividly when she first lay down, but they're faded now. Stumbling to the kitchen, she starts the coffee and stares at the painting hanging on the wall. *I painted that,* she thinks, trying to remember what it was like to sit down and pour all her energy into a single project.

"Mommy, color with me!" He pulls out his Transformer coloring book and a box of crayons, and they put their heads together and begin to fill in the image as the coffee percolates. His page is a mess of scribbles; hers intricately filled in with details.

"Wow . . ." His breath comes sweet and warm against her cheek. "You're a really pretty colorer, Mommy," he says. She smiles, choosing right there and then to believe that these precious moments are every bit as beautiful as the masterpiece on the wall. And that's art—the realization that this sweet creation, leaning forward on his elbows, is today's glorious offering, and so she gives it her full attention. And yet, as she swirls cream and sugar into her Ethiopian roast, she dreams quietly of a future day.

> The feeling I have inside of me is like a gentle weaving, a vibrating, a beating of wings, quivering in repose, holding of breath. When I am really able to paint, I shall paint that.
> Paula Modersohn-Becker, January 19, 1899

In the last chapter we learned that our call out into the world begins for us at home. Making sure our gospel love is clearly communicated there is our first priority. Our desire is that this love is also well received in every heart that enters through the front door, joins us round the table, or chats with us fireside. From this point on we will consider together when and how our artistic influence might expand beyond these four walls—beyond our figurative Jerusalem.

Though this book casts a vision of what this journey may look like, there is no formula to fit all our mothering days. That said, at some point in time, and perhaps you're already there, you may feel a Holy

Spirit push to move forward in your creative calling. The dormant years give way to a new phase of motherhood.

Some women make their way beyond that front porch swing in the midst of birthing more babies, but for many others this happens around the time the children head to school. As those stolen slivers of time become larger chunks, you tentatively take your first creative steps beyond that front porch swing. Inspiration comes fast like a fire hose for some, and fleeting as goose bumps for others. But whether she bellows loud or softly sings, inspiration is beckoning forward.

> Inspiration comes fast like a fire hose for some, and fleeting as goose bumps for others. But whether she bellows loud or softly sings, inspiration is beckoning forward.

Dropping your child off for three hours of preschool two days a week, you earmark those minutes, "Creative Me," then get to the business of living it. You rush home, stopping at a curbside stand for a celebratory bouquet of flowers. Walking through the front door, you slide the windows wide open, stick your daylilies into one of your good vases, and pull the old diaper-changing station back out of the garage, because we're talking about a new life. Yours!

Thus begins your transformation. Those drawers, which once held fresh diapers, are now repurposed to cradle color-coordinated sheets of craft paper and twine. Placing it against the empty wall in the laundry room, and hanging a sheet of cork above it all, you christen it your workstation and smile at the "dream board" where colors, textures, and pictures will be pinned for inspiration and direction in the days to come. You laugh out loud because there's work to be done, and you're just the girl for the job. You're inspired to get your hands in the clay, in the flour, in the fabrics, in the words once again.

After all the years when characters existed only in your mind, they'll now tumble onto the page and begin to take up residence. The hours spent dreaming of new curtains and fresh color will now become swatches of fabric and paint samples, and tomorrow will adorn your living room walls. That's Creative You, coming back to life again from the metaphorical dark ages. And it feels good. No, it feels *marvelous!*

When you return to pick your children up from school, take notice of your joy, and skip. No one's watching. Or maybe everyone's watching. *Skip anyway.* Let the joy of your creative hours propel you into refreshed relationship with your family. And as you sign them out of their classes and see that volunteer request for help with crafts or snacks, consider saying yes. Not to everything—you need room to bring that dream board to life—but to the things that fire you up. This may be your first tentative step out of Jerusalem and into Judea. Whether it's baking holiday muffins for a class party or writing up a newsletter and organizing park dates for the class, use your unique life to share gospel love with those around you.

Judea Needs a Room Mom

There's always that one mother who seems heaven-designed to be "Class Parent." She can rock a holiday party for twenty-two kindergarteners with more creative joy than the rest of the parents combined. That's my friend Angie.

Homeschooling three days a week and taking her children to a traditional school setting the other two, Angie uses her creativity both at home and on the children's campus. She brings literature to life on her family couch and laughs her way through the funniest journal entries that her children share. Then comes the reminder that tomorrow is the 100th day of school and she's whipping up sugar cookies, decorated like hundred dollar bills.

From her red, white, and blue layered flag cake when the students master the pledge of allegiance, to frosting-covered Christmas trees and springtime wind socks, Angie is gospel light at her children's school from September to May year after year. And when she's not serving in her local community, she's pinning pictures and recipes and posting to her blog, *Celebrating Holidays*, the online vehicle that carries Angie's light from her home and her community out into the world.

From one simple blog Angie inspires women to creatively celebrate life with their own children, focusing primarily on the holidays with a faith emphasis, like Thanksgiving, Christmas, St. Patrick's Day, and the Fourth of July. This is her passion and her unique calling both within and beyond her home.

Bridges

Just like Angie, you too have the power to influence and impact the world via the bridge of your creative gifts, from the confines of your own home. For the homebound artist, blogs, ebooks, and online shops are bridges. Suspension bridges, hung from heaven itself, connecting you with the world. Indeed, one of the greatest joys of blogging or selling one's designs online is the human connection component. When we receive a comment or an order from another person half a world away, suddenly the Great Commission becomes ordinary and possible, even tangible.

Before I had kids, the Great Commission conjured up images of treks to Papua New Guinea, or China, or maybe even our own inner city. But today, *the world is coming to us.*

Social media offers us the opportunity to interact with people in the farthest corners of the globe. We're simply women reaching out into the world with toddlers on our hips, pre-schoolers at our heels, and bellies growing babies. This is the draw of social media for creative moms today, all of us with pent-up inspiration looking for an outlet. Board after board of Pinterest ideas bombard us, enticing our creative sensibilities back to life again.

> For the homebound artist, blogs, ebooks, and online shops are bridges. Suspension bridges, hung from heaven itself, connecting you with the world.

Have you seen the way art is shooting like fireworks from the narrow sliver-spaces of other busy, creative mamas? Shining through handcrafted Christmas gifts, from whimsical Instagram photos of family life, Facebook posts of renovated bedside tables, and blogs filled with poetry and prose about children, marriage, and faith. In this digitally powered Great Awakening of the arts, creativity is finding its own way out like deep magic working itself free.

A mother's artistry spills out through the cracks and crevices, the seemingly stolen moments of her mothering days. And as children grow up into their independence, and in the larger spaces of school days, she finds a new rhythm.

Little girl legs in summer shorts lay bare against the red vinyl upholstery of Grandma's kitchen bench. Sticky and spent from the heat, she leans over the table, learning the art of making letters. Not the simple ABC's that you and I learned, but the scripted swirls that trail from a calligraphy pen.

Lyn made countless swooping letters when she was young. However, more than art, Lyn made memories. There beside her grandma, amidst the smells and sounds of family, this antiquated art form found a home in the deep recesses of her DNA. But time moved on, and Lyn grew up, and before long she had a family of her own, and the years practicing calligraphy all seemed to be a thing of the past as she pursued other dreams.

During this season with two young sons underfoot, Lyn preserved her femininity and artistic nature by making pretty things around their house. Handcrafted invitations to her children's birthday parties, lovingly sewn tea cozies for preschool teachers, and a banner over her mantel to herald each new season. Tucked away in the confines of her home, all that her grandma had taught Lyn began to bubble up again, flowing unhindered at last from delicate fingertips.

During nap times and playdates and long evening hours when her husband traveled for work, Lyn created. She was private about it from the beginning and laughed self-consciously when friends suggested she turn her passion into a business. After all, life was busy, and her art was blessing her own small circle of family and friends. For Lyn that was enough.

After nine intense years with babies and preschoolers filling most every ounce of her full-cup days, the last child ventured off to school. And when he did, all this art and beauty filling the corners of her home and imagination spilled naturally over into a career.

Today Lyn sells her authentic handmade works of art from her online shop, Lyn Anderson Designs. Special orders for wedding announcements, nursery art, and favorite Scriptures roll in steadily, and when there's a lull she dabbles in illustration and watercolor. But at two o'clock each Monday through Friday, when her iPhone alarm sings loud, Lyn carefully tucks away each pen and hangs parchment sheets to dry. She washes ink spots from her hands, grabs her keys, and heads out the door to pick up the kids from school.

When they return home the slow cooker simmers and its aroma greets them at the door. The children run to the eight-foot chalkboard, hanging wide like an embrace above the dining room table. White swirls stretch long and inviting: *Beef Stew and Crusty French Bread.* And the children cheer as they anticipate dinner.

Learning to set healthy boundaries around our work time is important as we move out into the world. Though the Internet never really turns off its lights, we Renaissance moms must learn to close up shop for the day. We *must.* In this fast-paced, digital society that never slumbers, we must unplug in order to plug into family life. The glory of it all is that we can do this faith and family life with art mashed up tight against us, all rolled together, like Lyn's decorative signs announcing that night's menu. Life and art, together. But it takes intentionality. You know that, and so do I.

All for the Cross

Of course the apostles didn't live out this Great Commission call via any social media device. It was simply *social*—hands and feet and meals around the table. They didn't tweet it, pin it, upload it. They didn't whip up a fresh batch of homemade caramels sprinkled in sea salt, wrapped up in butcher's paper with a great big bow. But those first missionaries *are* our examples of what it means to take the love and light of Christ out into the world. Here's the difference, creative mom: the early disciples walked on Roman roads, while you walk in the fullness of your creativity.

> God can use your creative bent to bend others toward the cross.

Whatever your talents, God can use your creative bent to bend others toward the cross. All He asks of us is that we give the totality of our lives back to Him. Every dream, every gifting, every day. Oh the irony of it. You do not have to "give up your art," dear mom, but you must give it all up to Him. And isn't that what defines the consecrated Christian life—the life devoted to God? So we sing this treasured hymn anew:

> Take my life and let it be consecrated, Lord, to Thee.
> Take my moments and my days, let them flow in ceaseless praise.
> Take my hands and let them move at the impulse of Thy love.
> Take my feet and let them be swift and beautiful for Thee.
>
> Frances R. Havergal, 1874

Marvelous books have already been written about the consecrated Christian life, but we are focusing on the unique, offered-up reality of a creative mom, and our song tumbles out sacrificially: take my painting and let it be . . . take my camera and let it be . . . take my baking and let it be . . . take my designing . . . my crafting . . . my writing . . . my mothering . . . and let it all be *ever, only all for Thee.*

Missy was a simple mom, living her life in quiet pursuit of the Lord when He captured her heart on a crisp April morning. She heard His voice almost audibly speak to her soul. *"I've got a daughter who needs to know I still love her."* Shaken and compelled to act, Missy spoke with her husband, and within days they had signed up and agreed to bring a Ukrainian teenager into their home for the summer through an orphan-hosting program.

Over the course of five weeks, Missy and her family poured into this young girl. They broke through the language barrier thanks to translation apps, reminding her over and over that she was loved, that her life held worth in this world.

Before sending her home, Missy longed to give her something that she could take back with her, something that would be a visual reminder God valued and loved her. Knowing that this young woman would be sent back to a place where she had little evidence of her identity and worth, Missy wanted to place a tangible expression in the palms of her hands.

Late one evening, Missy sat in the corner of her couch, praying and seeking the Lord for ways to give the young girl in her home a deep and abiding understanding of His great love for her—one that transcended language barriers. That's when she remembered the sparrow.

Moving to her daughter's room, she pulled the tiny clay sparrow off the shelf and moved it through her fingers. Made out of a simple lump of polymer clay, with a penny pressed into its underbelly, this sparrow represented so much of God's grace.

> Are not two sparrows sold for a cent? And yet not one of them will fall to the ground apart from your Father. But the very hairs of your head are all numbered. So do not fear; you are more valuable than many sparrows. (Matt. 10:29–31)

One little sparrow. The thought came down as quickly as her prayer ascended. The next morning, Missy delicately placed the clay sparrow into her host daughter's hand and awkwardly translated the words, "When you look at this bird, remember that we love you and so does God."

This small act birthed a creative ministry Missy ran for a season from her home. Her mission, both in her mothering and in her creative endeavors, is to raise awareness for orphans throughout the world while reminding every woman (every daughter) that they are valued beyond measure by a Father in Heaven who knows them by name, created them intentionally, and loves them unconditionally.

Missy contacted the original creator of the small sparrow that adorned her daughter's room and asked permission to continue making similar treasures in order to raise money and awareness for hurting hearts. Once Missy began molding clay in the palms of her hands, something else broke open deep inside of her. Creativity. A part of Missy's unique creative design split open and spilled forth into hundreds of other new ideas. From the confines of a mother's heart and home, God's love began pouring out into the world in creative ways.

This is the gospel, all rolled up in polymer clay by the tender, loving hands of a mother sitting at her dining room table. This is the impact of a Renaissance mom. Her creative skills may seem ordinary, and her life so very unglamorous, but to the fatherless child, the gift is extraordinary. God is shining His love through the simple acts of creative surrender from humble homes.

Many of you are taking the literal gospel message of faith in Christ out into the world through story and song. Some of you are using your gifts to simply make relationships, with the hope of spreading God's relational love. And others of you are giving away the profits you've made from your creative endeavors to support missionaries, feed the poor, and care for orphans. What thrilling opportunities we have to partner in the Great Commission in this modern age. Ministries are popping up all over the world, fueled by the creative power of ordinary extraordinary women, many of them mothers, all bent on taking this gospel message of love to a hurting people.

When we start to converse, creative to creative, about the impact we can have on the world as a whole, all sorts of ideas start to run. Of course this going out will look different for each one of us. Our songs will carry a different tune, our brushstrokes all unique, the prayers we cry out, and the mercy ministries we partner with will all differ because of our glorious distinctiveness and the way the Spirit prompts each heart.

Every mother was made to care for her family, but she was also made to care for the world. And never was there an easier time for women to journey out to the farthest corners of the globe than in this digital age, with the power of art at the helm of her ship.

God made you for the world, and commissioned you to go.

Chapter Four

Renaissance Faire

The most ancient expression of creativity began not in notes and scales but in the formation of life.... God's creative work binds together your life with your purpose to sing new songs that connect to the Creator's original score. Your life continues adding notes to the original melody.

Sean Cooper

Reaching back, I found the microphone pack attached to my skirt band and flipped the switch on. Just offstage I gently grasped a handful of heavy velvet curtain, closed my eyes, and listened as the soloist sang her piece. It was the song I had asked her to sing before they introduced me. The lyrics so perfectly set up the topic I would be teaching on that night, and the gentle vibrato of her voice effortlessly filled the room, giving testimony to the fact that *she was created for this*.

Peeking out between a thin crack in the dark curtains I glimpsed His radiance on her face; her throat an open conduit, her creative life an emphatic *yes* to how God made her.

For we are His workmanship, created in Christ Jesus for good works, which God prepared beforehand so that we would walk in them. (Eph. 2:10)

In the days that followed, Ephesians 2:10 rang like a bell from somewhere deep within. This verse, hidden for years in my heart, came to life in a profound new way as I watched that beautiful singer step fully into who she was made to be. I guess I believed it was true—that we each have good works to discover in this labyrinth of life—but suddenly the reality of that truth wasn't an elusive game of hide-and-go-seek. It was then I began to believe that God purposefully, intentionally, designed us to walk in the good works He had prepared from the beginning of time. And for the creative, the imagery only gets better, because our good works are often works of art.

workmanship (*noun*). The thing which is made, designed, crafted, or created.

Workmanship, while easy for all to understand, pales in comparison to the New Living Translation's *masterpiece.* Yes, the hands of the true Master of heaven and earth masterfully crafted us individually for good works. And when the good works are works of art then we might go so far as to say, the Master created us as masterpieces, that we might create masterpieces to reflect the Master! Chew on that one slowly now.

masterpiece (*noun*). A work of artistic expression that is done with such extraordinary skill as to make it stand out among others like it and worthy to be emulated.

But the original Greek text is even better: *poiēma,* from which we derive the English word *poem.* We are God's Poems written to the world. Poems cased in flesh, penned in red with His own Son's blood. Written by the Master's own hand. Every stanza a good work. Each rhyming couplet the cadence as we walk in them. Every story, every song, every picture, every thread, every party, every scarf sold to benefit an orphan in need . . . all predestined good works.

Poiēma, you were not casually created by God with an artistic bent, then set free to wander and to wonder what for. Though seasons may feel confusing, the Lord knew exactly what He was doing when He created you creative. He designed you intentionally artistic, and then set you free for good purposes.

> Your eyes saw my unformed body;
> all the days ordained for me were written in your book
> before one of them came to be. (Ps. 139:16 NIV)

But surely it's not easy here in our metaphorical Jerusalem with so many hearts to train and meals to serve, checkbooks to balance, the love-fire in a marriage that always need stoking, and rooms that explode in a fresh mess each day. It's not easy to find the time to create from your treasure store of inspiration. As you dip your hands into the scorching dishwater late at night to scrub the pots clean, perhaps you wonder if you might have missed one of those good creative works in the busyness of motherhood.

> The Master created us as masterpieces, that we might create masterpieces to reflect the Master!

Halfway through that thought a child wanders out of her room and into the kitchen, and you usher her back to bed again with another kiss and a glass of water. No, to everything there is a season, and in this season your good works have been at home with the children. Or perhaps you're splitting the time, because you're needed in the workforce in order that you might help provide. Tonight may not be the night you get your project done (or even started) but for the *poiēma* who is also a mother, this needs to be okay. Disappointing sometimes, but okay—because you, dear mother, are a work of art!

God didn't purpose our creative lives to simply make things of beauty; our lives themselves God has made altogether beautiful.

You with your messy imperfections, your dirty floors and over-whelmed schedule, your date nights dressing up for your husband in a clean pair of yoga pants, and your family movie nights sprawled on the couch laughing as Tom chases Jerry. When the pottery wheel hasn't spun for a month of Sundays, you are still His walking, talking masterpiece. No barren season can take that away. Though you haven't finished the blog post you promised yourself you would, you remain the living, breathing story of a redeemed life, pushing her child on a swing. And the days spent working nine to five aren't a waste of your creative gifts either, because they too are part of a sweeping portrait, an epic poem. *His.*

Though you think yourself the painter, you are the canvas.

Though you see yourself the decorator, you are most beautifully designed.

Though you pen a thousand melodies, you are the song.

Though you consider yourself the potter, you are the sculpture.

Though you fancy yourself the messenger, you are the message.

Though you are tempted to measure your worth in what you create, *it is enough merely that you were created.*

It was an art festival in the middle of summer with glass blowers, children's exhibits, and live music. We walked amid row upon row of displays, marveling at the thick globs of oil that lifted two inches off the canvas, flowers blooming forward so realistic they were nearly fragrant. I stopped at one booth and remarked how like the Italian Riviera the painting was, and the artist, with dark Mediterranean eyes and broken English, said, "This is the view from my home."

Down the lane, a gigantic picture of a pink elephant made me laugh out loud until I cried, "She makes me happy!" And a jovial woman my mother's age, sitting in a canvas chair nearby, leapt up and cried out, "She makes me happy too!" And I commended her for her bravery in daring to make something so strange and wonderful.

A little farther still, a man as large as the sun sat on a three-legged stool. His hair was long, tied back in a red braid. He wore a kilt and sat with his knees apart, which made me blush. And the whole earth seemed to gather there and watch him weave leather strips into intricate jewelry. My husband smiled and put his arm around me, like he knew what I was thinking about that behemoth of a man. "I love creative people so much," I whispered, and he nodded.

These men and women are the clay work of God. And with their unique artistry, their humor, their joys, their sorrows, and their natural earth materials, they adorn the world with beauty. But my heart wasn't moved by *their* creativity nearly as much as the understanding that they were, each one, a picture of *His* creativity. Masterpieces weaving a tale of the Master Creator as they sculpted, sang, and made intricate lace patterns with their own two hands.

His Art.

His Masterpiece.

His *Poiēma*.

Adorning the Word

While the picture of the flowers, and the one of the pink elephant, and those woven bracelets made by the laughing giant all decorate our *lives* with beauty, there is other art and there are other artists who adorn the world with the very gospel itself. And the marriage of the two is a holy ceremony.

As my husband and I walked along the far side of the art festival thinking we had seen all there was to see, I came upon her display. Though set upon the same white backdrop, her work was altogether different. Brushstrokes made images pop like a perfectly lit photograph, stopping all who passed by. I, however, was arrested by something entirely different. The words pulled at my heart, there beside the image of an African woman carrying bananas on her head. "She girds herself with strength and strengthens her arms."

Artist after artist lined the walkways, but Hannah Harris stood apart from all the others. Her work was faith based, often including fragmented pieces of Scripture, always celebrating God's intrinsic love for humanity. There were no pictures of crosses, only images of people; not outright Scripture complete with references, but Scripture truth displayed in a phrase, and sometimes merely the childlike faith bound up in a subject's eye, each one unique and inspired.

Subtly, Hannah communicated her faith on canvas, comfortable and welcoming, and not at all exclusive. Those paintings, and the artist herself, were a beautiful picture of the call we all have on our lives to share Christ in ways that make our neighbors, family, coworkers, and friends feel comfortable *and curious*. Hannah's art does that—like a sort of friendship, inviting everyone into her picture, regardless of his or her faith. Yet faith is present, an underlying conversation just waiting to happen.

Today, an army of artists creates faith-inspired and faith-inspiring art. Designing graphics out of Scriptures and songs. Jess Connolly is one who has christened her baby's nap times as her own personal space and place for the glory-crash of faith and art. At first it was only a few canvases covered in Scripture to adorn the walls of her home. Then she gave a couple of pieces to friends and sold a few others. It was the most natural transition a creative mom could have. Then all of a sudden, in those precious quiet hours, a business was born. She named her company *Naptime Diaries*.

Jess was simply a mom in the middle of motherhood—"just a gal in the thick of it herself" is how she describes it. But thick or thin, with ample room to create or very little at all, Jess's inspiration was clear and strong—to adorn the world with the gospel message of Christ. When it was time to sum it all up with a tagline for her blog, this is what she wrote: *Creatively write Scripture on the walls of your heart + home.*

Over the last few years, with children growing and a marriage deepening, Jess has shipped thousands of prints and canvases to adorn the walls of homes the world over. From within the protection of her own holy Jerusalem, Jess's creative offering has reached the farthest corners of the globe. And the gospel impact has had a multiplying effect. Not only is Jess communicating creatively with Scripture, she's inspiring other artisans to do likewise. Mom-artists are creating graphics on websites and decals on nursery walls, lyrics to old hymns over the dining room table, and tee shirts boasting faith in fashionable ways.

The Melding of Art and Faith

For many creative Christians, art and faith are *obviously* intertwined, their artistry spilling forth in a visual gospel display. But for others, this is a very real struggle—not knowing how art and faith should blend. When art doesn't give a blatant visual representation of Christ in every stroke of the paintbrush, completed manuscript, or belted-out song, we tend to wonder if it's good enough. Is it all right? Is there a place for creative Christians who aren't producing overtly Christian work?

The auditorium was packed that afternoon, hundreds of literary hopefuls, avid readers, admiring law students, and simple fans all squeezed in together to hear one of the most respected and prolific writers of our time tell his story. It was 2000, my senior year, and my eyes gleamed with all the hopes and potential of publication. So when I heard that John Grisham would be coming to speak on campus, I jumped at the opportunity to hear him.

I loved Mr. Grisham's story. It took him three years to write *A Time to Kill*, and two years to secure an agent. The novel was picked up by a small publishing house that ordered only five thousand copies printed. Grisham bought one thousand of those and sold them himself.

Meager beginnings from a man who just had stories to tell.

At the end of his talk, Grisham opened the floor for a Q and A. This started off nicely with students asking smart, respectful questions. Then a girl stepped to the mic and opened a can of worms with a simple inquiry.

"Mr. Grisham," she said, "thank you for speaking with us today. I noticed you spoke of your faith, and yet I can't help but wonder why, if you believe yourself to be a Christian, you aren't writing Christian books that are more God-honoring."

Grisham paused and looked closely at the girl, an amused smile tilting his mouth upward. He cleared his throat and leaned forward just a little before speaking. "Well," he began. "The reason is simple. I am a Christian who is a writer. I'm not a Christian writer." He straightened up and took a sip of water as the audience erupted in applause.

> Urge bondslaves to be subject to their own masters in everything, to be well-pleasing, not argumentative, not pilfering, but showing all good faith *so that they will adorn the doctrine of God our Savior in every respect.* (Titus 2:9–10)

Or, as the King James Version says, ". . . that they may adorn the doctrine of God our Saviour *in all things.*" We adorn His message of salvation by how we live our lives—with our pleasing words and our actions, our honesty and integrity. Not how we paint a picture of Jesus on a literal canvas, but how we live that picture of "Christ in us" every day. In this way we adorn the doctrine of God in *every respect.*

> **adorn** (*verb*). Decorate. To make something even more attractive by adding something beautiful to it.

Christian artists are doing amazing work, adorning homes around the world with the literal doctrine of faith, the Word of God. And moms every day are uploading portraits of their children, adding a family verse, then hanging them on living room walls as a decorative statement of faith. Jewelry makers are hand-stamping verses into leather cuffs. Others of you find yourself more in Grisham's camp. And so we pose the question: Must the secular and the sacred be separated at all?

When we are gracious ambassadors of God's love for mankind, *we* adorn His message *in all things.* His light shines from our lives, penetrating every corner of the world by the way we live, and not just via the canvases we hang on the wall. *We* are the canvases, making God in us look good! That's when we decorate His message of love. That's when we adorn the gospel, making it beautiful to the people in our sphere of influence.

Let's read it again in another version:

> Teach slaves to be subject to their masters in everything, to try to please them, not to talk back to them, and not to steal from them, but to show that they can be fully trusted, *so that in every way they will make the teaching about God our Savior attractive.* (Titus 2:9–10 NIV)

In this passage, Paul is telling Titus what to teach the people in the early church of Crete. The message is short, but he includes this missive to slaves, that they are to be subject to their masters. I used to stumble over this verse awkwardly because it has to do with slavery and the subjection of the weak under the rule of an oppressor. But I have come to see how God uses this imagery of slaves and a master to show us our relationship with Him. You and I serve a Holy Master; we are handmaidens to the King of all creation. And here's the kicker: what our Master wants is hearts that have integrity whether we are working in the secular or the sacred. When we live out our faith consistently, no matter what we do or where we go, we make Him look good. It is in how we live that we have the greatest power to make His gospel attractive, in every way.

Not to say that our artistry isn't part of His reflection in our lives. For God is the Creator, the Word from the very beginning of time, the painter of this world and all that is in it, the rhythm to which we sing, and the measured beat of every poem. Therefore, since we are His created beings, fashioned in His image, all forms of creativity have the *potential* to point to Him. The *poiēma*,

> Therefore, since we are His created beings, fashioned in His image, all forms of creativity have the *potential* to point to Him.

therefore, testifies of the Poet by the very nature of her creativity, and then also by her gentle and kind spirit. The unique quality of her artistry mingles with the Christlike qualities of her life, and the two flow naturally out into the world together.

> Your adornment must not be merely external—braiding the hair, and wearing gold jewelry, or putting on dresses; but let it be the hidden person of the heart, with the imperishable quality of a gentle and quiet spirit, which is precious in the sight of God. (1 Peter 3:3–4)

And so we return to the questions posed earlier: Must the sacred and secular be separated? What do you do when your creative genius doesn't splash out as a visual gospel display upon the wall? What of the Christian woman whose art doesn't give a literal representation of Christ? Is there something missing? Absolutely not! For we are His created—testifying in all we say, in all we do, in all we create.

His Art.

His Masterpiece.

His *Poiēma*.

You *are* the gospel, the portrait of a saved life, bearing light in your home, there in your local community, and out into the world in the way you do business. That is enough. As God's redeemed daughter, you are perfectly marvelous exactly how God made you and through the exact medium of however He inspires you today.

> Whatever you do in word or deed [or artistry], do all in the name of the Lord Jesus, giving thanks through Him to God the Father. (Col. 3:17)

Amy is a wife and mother, a woman of deep faith and, to top it off, a baker. She doesn't just bake for fun either. Kneading flour and sugar and all the other heavenly ingredients together, Amy creates works of art in cookie form. And her art tastes as good as it looks.

As the master baker behind her own cookie company, Amy's creativity is both an outlet and a way to help provide for her family. She doesn't just make cookies; she makes a living right there in her kitchen. But make no mistake, what Amy does is the work of an artist. It took her awhile to see that. For a long time, if you asked Amy about her art, she would shy away, embarrassed because she felt that what she did held little value. "It felt so . . . *froofy*," she told me over coffee one balmy Wednesday morning. "I see the value in great writing and music and art, but a plate full of cookies? It just felt silly, like it didn't have any weight."

It's true that we often see the faith impact in a well-penned poem or in the powerful refrain of our favorite song, but we should not dismiss the impact that we can similarly have through the creative gifts of hospitality. When Amy shows up at an event with a plate of cookies that she's spent hours baking and decorating, the receivers of her delectable art are blessed. Blessed by her art, and blessed by her heart. Her art decorates their party, but it is her heart that adorns and beautifies the gospel in their midst!

> Some titles sit somewhat naturally. I teach—I'm a teacher. I raise children—I'm a mom.
>
> We don't seem to wrestle with the obvious ones, the ones that people can't wager an opinion on. . . .
>
> It's different with art. How many of us are willing to call ourselves artists? We're waiting for that mystical qualifier. Sometimes, we're waiting for a particular person to crown us with the title, too timid to claim it ourselves. Afraid of seeming prideful. Afraid of being discounted, busy outlining our numerous disqualifying factors.
>
> Kris Camealy

Is *artist* a title that makes you squirm a bit? Are you afraid that you haven't earned the right to bear the moniker? I remember years of waiting for someone to just give me a chance to show the world what I was capable of as an artist. Once I had the validation of a big job, then I could join the ranks, but until that time I felt like I was simply sneaking into a party uninvited.

What eventually changed for me was the realization of whose party it was. God is the one throwing this artistic celebration online today, and every single one of us is invited. Not just the ladies who make an income from their offerings, not simply the ones who have successful Etsy shops or thousands of followers on Instagram, but every one of us who reflects the Master Creator by embracing creativity in our own unique way is invited to our Renaissance Faire in this diverse digital age.

You are His Poem. Your heart and your art are His song to the world. *Sing it loud.*

Chapter Five

Our Most Beautiful Creations

I thought of Nanny, and how she'd missed the art that was her children, right in front of her, for all of her wanting to be an artist.

How she'd missed the beauty in the lines of her children's jaws, in the swinging of their arms, in the graceful dance of their limbs.

And I picked up Aiden, almost reverently, said into his wide unblinking eyes, "You are my greatest creation."

Emily T. Wierenga

It's early. The darkness of night has yet to be chased away by the new morning's light. Once again, I sit at my desk and stare out the glass door in front of me into the vacuous black.

Black like the slick ink that fills my pen.

The sleek black of a baby grand.

The half-used tube of your blackest oil paint.

The black velvet lining of your instrument case.

Of course there's a small part of me that wishes I were still wrapped tight in my bed. But I pulled myself from the warm cocoon before sleep had fully left my eyes not because I *wanted* to, but because I *needed* to. Inspiration beckons me. Many nights as I attempt sleep, I feel words like dreams swimming through my soul, and they call me from slumber. Such is the life of a creative mom, with self-expression fighting its way free. I didn't always have to steal the night hours in order to create. Creative self-expression used to arrive on her own timetable, rising up and out of me whenever she felt so inclined.

I read a story once of a woman, a poet, who walked about her father's field midday. Without warning she felt the earth beneath her feet begin to shake, like a railroad train was coming her way. She sensed it in the air, all around her, this massive thing moving toward her. Only instead of a train, she knew instinctively that this thing was a poem she needed to catch fast before it passed her by. Desperate for a pencil to capture the inspiration barreling down upon her, she tore through the field, fierce and fast, as the roar of words caught up to her, breathing steam at her neck. Tearing through the farmhouse, up the stairs, and to her room, she reached for a pencil and paper to record the words that begged to be written. Sometimes she'd make it in time to catch the wave, the poem tumbling off the tips of her fingers, dotting the page with beauty. Other times, however, she missed the wind of inspiration as it rushed right through her before pencil met paper.

I get chills when I envision that girl running wild for her house, hair flying, trying to catch the words before they thundered past. I know that dreadful, wonderful sensation of inspiration coming down hard. However, I am not a child anymore, not barefoot in my father's field, not free to run whenever I'm inspired—run for a pen, for my laptop, camera, paintbrush, pottery wheel, guitar. No, now I am a mother with children of my own to tend.

To drop what I'm doing for the sake of a song, a picture, or the perfectly nuanced first line to a short story isn't always possible. Sometimes it is, but other times running off would mean leaving my kids behind, forsaking that precious sanctified time that I set aside so carefully.

Missing the baseball game and the field trip, the long-promised walk to the park and a lemonade stand. And so, instead of running each time inspiration bids me come, I pull back the covers, plant my feet on the cold tile floor, start the coffee maker, and pray the Lord sends the inspired muse upon me then, in the only quiet I'm afforded each day.

I vividly remember the first time I saw the movie *The Secret Garden*. I was ten, and immediately upon finishing the film I took a notebook and a pen and walked into the woods that stood just beyond our Wisconsin property. I found the nearest tree with thick, strong limbs, and climbed as high as I dared. Looking into the maze of branches and leaves, I penned a short poem. Back then my art was whimsical and fresh. Stories danced like fairies through my imagination, and all I needed to create was a tall tree, a colored pen, and a blank page.

There's Magic Still to Be Found

Today the art is seemingly more confined and life less whimsical, and yet the children in my midst remind me daily that there is still magic to be found in a tree with sturdy branches, a movie that inspires a scribbled sonnet, and the shapes of clouds begging for interpretation. Slowly, I'm learning that whimsy is still as present today as it was in my youth, here in the laughter of my loved ones. Sure, I can't always climb a tree or run up the stairs to my room for a pen, but I can live, most assuredly, this inspired life with them.

There is much inspiration to be found in the imaginations of our own children. Not yet bogged down by the responsibilities of life, their senses are attuned to the world in a way that we have long forgotten. A few

> The children in my midst remind me daily that there is still magic to be found in a tree with sturdy branches . . . and the shapes of clouds begging for interpretation.

summers back, I took my little clan to the beach to soak up the perfect warmth of a glorious day. As we sat in the sand grabbing handfuls of grapes from the picnic basket, I asked them to close their eyes and tell me what they heard. Their words were magic and as they spoke, eyes squinted shut tight, I quickly pulled out my iPhone and recorded their responses. Because that moment was art.

> I hear nothing.
> Oh. The ocean.
> People screaming and those girls
> Saying "hahaha . . ."
>
> Waves crashing
> And splashing
> Seagulls cawing
> And laughing.
> Happy voices.

When I made a keepsake book of pictures at the end of summer, each child's words decorated a page. Years from now, when we glance back through those memories, I will remember the art of that sunny day, the way their blond hair whipped me in the face as I leaned in for salty kisses, and how the seagulls laughed amidst the happiness of it all. But I also recall the fatigue that followed our day in the sun, how utterly worn out I was from the exertion. My husband had been traveling for two weeks straight and the kitchen was a pile of dishes, the laundry room a pile of clothes, and sand crunched beneath my feet as I walked from room to room

> Embrace the magic in the mundane and you embrace the most beautiful creations in your midst.

dropping good-night kisses. A magical day followed by a bone-weary night, and no time in between.

Here we are again, painting pictures of this Renaissance life in all its manifold splendor, to remind our hearts that this present season is not devoid of creativity. It is, in fact, fertile ground for tomorrow's masterpiece. Embrace the magic in the mundane and you embrace the most beautiful creations in your midst.

The woman pulled my traveling companion aside and, with a generous smile, presented her with a gift. Vibrant swaths of fabric made right there in her own village. Through a translator, she gave the present with a charge: "Make something beautiful."

We were in Tanzania for a weeklong glimpse into the work of Compassion International. A ragtag group of writers, interior decorators, photographers, and handmade crafters, partnering together to use our unique gifts to proclaim the message of compassion and care out into the world. Every one of us had left children behind for this weeklong adventure—every one of us but one. Maggie Whitley was not yet a mom, though she

> Creative women hold their art like a living, breathing thing.

cradled that fabric like a mother holds her newborn babe. And we all swayed side to side beside her, tenderly rocking, because we all understood: creative women hold their art like a living, breathing thing.

As that Tanzanian woman placed her brightly colored bolt of fabric into Maggie's hands, the journey became so much more than simply telling the stories of people we encountered. Suddenly we all saw the village through Maggie's eyes as we walked red dirt roads. At nearly every turn, there were men and women sitting outside at sewing machines, children by their side as they wove fabric into beautiful creations. As we strolled by, they looked up and waved, and it always seemed they saved their sweetest smiles for Maggie, as though there were an unspoken camaraderie with this seamstress from the other side of the world.

Once back in her home, Maggie took the fabric so graciously given to her and did not disappoint in her ability to "make something beautiful."

Fashioning a unique collection of handmade zippered pouches, she sold them in her popular online shop, *Gussy Sews*, and then used the proceeds to sponsor a young girl from Tanzania.

The rest of our team all returned home to bustling family lives. Children had so much to share and husbands collapsed, grateful to have their wives back again. In the hours we were able to pull away from our loved ones, we crafted stories and uploaded photos from our time in Tanzania. Blog posts carried the charge for readers to sponsor more children from the Compassion International program, and all the while Maggie's sewing machine hummed.

An experience like the one Maggie had in Tanzania leaves a lasting mark, both on the woman and on the world. However, God had more in store for this young gal with the creative heart, for shortly after returning home Maggie discovered that her life path would soon change. It all started when she saw two pink lines.

One year after our trip to Tanzania, Maggie and her husband, Zack, welcomed their son into the world, and life and art and faith intermingled in a new way. Where once her days flowed seamlessly to the rhythmic whir of her sewing machine, now they were dictated by the precious cries of a blond-haired babe with a smile that split wide his face, and her heart. He was followed eighteen months later by a little sister, and less than a year after that, Maggie and her husband received another surprise as two pink lines showed up yet again. And all at once the priorities that had dictated Maggie's days seemed unimportant next to the bundles in her arms.

> When a creative mom takes a hiatus from her art, the mom is still creative. Always has been. Always will be.

There was nothing she could make in those early days of childrearing that would compare to the wonder of these swaddled creations. And so Maggie stepped back from her art for a time. Those beautiful, custom handbags and pouches—her creations—were placed appropriately on the back burner of importance so she could focus entirely on her most beautiful creations. What Maggie learned was that when a creative mom takes a hiatus from her art, the mom is still creative. Always has been. Always will be.

"Creating has always filled a need inside my soul," Maggie told me when we reconnected after the birth of her second child. "The art may not look the same right now, but the need to create hasn't changed. Creativity is as much in me now as it was in my past, and will be in my future. This is a part of who I am, and I'm open to seeing the art evolve."

The creativity that took Maggie half a world away just a few short years ago looks different today. Her art hasn't been sacrificed completely; it's simply changed shape with the ebb and flow of motherhood—a season that is difficult and exhausting, but also good. So very, very good. And beyond good, this early season of motherhood is *short*. In the blink of an eye, the days turn to months, and then years, and the time naturally lengthens, making way for the creative pulse to beat strong again. This is the natural progression of a creative mother's life.

Live It First

Dream dreams, then write them. Aye, but live them first.

Samuel Eliot Morison

I feel an urgency to live, to not miss out on these living years with my children at home for the sake of writing it all down. Because, you know, this is a dream too. A dream come true for so many of us, with the miracle family we hoped and prayed for. Still, there are other dreams, creative dreams, dreams of starting a business or working in women's ministry. Dreams of seeing our art impact lives outside our own four walls. So many dreams swell within.

And so we must look for ways to honor the art within us that don't require us to abandon the people around us. Especially in these intense seasons where simply living takes everything we've got! Young children, illnesses and behavior training, spouses who need us more than ever,

> We must look for ways to honor the art within us that don't require us to abandon the people around us.

work outside the home demanding more of our time than we had factored in, laundry and dishes and another trip to the grocery store—there are seasons when it simply isn't possible to pull away to feed the artist confined inside.

But take heart, the pendulum of the clock always swings back again. Finding its rhythm, finding its balance in the long marathon of life. For some intense sprints, there is no balance, and so we need a plan to carry our parched creative souls to the next watering hole.

> Then the LORD answered me and said,
> "Record the vision
> And inscribe it on tablets,
> That the one who reads it may run.
> For the vision is yet for the appointed time;
> It hastens toward the goal and it will not fail.
> Though it tarries, wait for it;
> For it will certainly come, it will not delay." (Hab. 2:2–3)

This often-skipped portion of the Old Testament is ripe with hope for the future day.

Creative mom, lean in just a bit closer here, because I've got a pearl for you to string and wear: just because God grants inspiration and vision for a story, a picture, a recipe, or even a retro A-line skirt, it doesn't necessarily mean *today* is the day to write and do and create it. Today may simply be the day for faith and patience and endurance—living the gospel out at home, in your own personal Jerusalem. At times such as these, let us cultivate the art of "recording the vision" by simply jotting it down as a note for tomorrow.

An older, wiser woman once encouraged me to keep a journal or a file of all the messages I'm inspired to one day write. Crafters, dressmakers, jewelry designers, bakers, home decorators, graphic designers . . . this is your Pinterest board. You're pinning and pining for the day that is hastening toward you so that the inspiration isn't lost in this season of blessed busyness.

If you are smack-dab in the middle of this intense season of mothering right now, and the idea of carving out even a little time for your craft overwhelms your heart and your family balance, then take this woman's wisdom to heart. Tuck away each torn-out picture from a magazine, each story concept, each personal revelation that supports your vision. Jot it down and file it away, then move about your day with peace in your heart that the inspiration waits for you. This recorded book of ideas opens wide the gift of freedom, allowing you to live your dreams first.

I know a young woman who understands the blessing of a good journal better than anyone else. She once had a blog. Unfortunately for me she doesn't share her words there anymore, because there simply isn't enough time to craft them for an audience. Today, when the words do come, she catches them upon the pages of her private journals. Mindy Rogers may one day write for the world again, but today she pours out her raw, unedited thoughts for an audience of One.

> I'm a collector of journals.
> I keep them stashed in the console of my car,
> tucked into the folds of my purse,
> laid on the shelf in my entryway,
> stacked by the jewelry box on my dresser,
> and sometimes pushed deep into the back pocket of my worn
>   out jeans.
> My husband makes jokes but the truth is that they are
>   everywhere.
> Every day I spill my heart out in ink on the paper of these
>   journals.
>
> Mindy Rogers

Mom to two darling girls, teacher, wife, and a passionate follower of Jesus—not necessarily in that order—this journal aficionado is catching inspiration in ink on paper, saving each line as fuel and fodder for another day, when the fullness of time comes upon her and a new season bids her write. She'll be ready.

> Journaling your inspiration is a gift. It says, "I trust that the future holds good things."

Journaling your inspiration is a gift. It says, "I trust that the future holds good things."

For many creative souls, inspiration floods late at night when the house grows still and the distractions of the day fade. As the light of the moon winks a story into your heart, grab the journal, pick up your laptop, pin your inspiration, record the raw melody on your iPhone, sketch the design, lay down the lyrics at the altar table of your journal's pages, then *sleep*. The rest will continue to fuel your creative soul, and it will give you the grace to focus fully on your most beautiful creations when they toddle to your bedside in the early morning hours.

Visions and inspiration can be all consuming, but don't worry about bringing them to fruition today, my friend. There is an appointed time; it hastens toward the goal and it will not fail. Though it tarries, wait for it; for it will certainly come. There is a time for visions, a time for dreams, a time for living, and a time to create. And the One who inspires is the same One who makes all things beautiful in His time.

> What sort of diary should I like mine to be? Something loose knit and yet not slovenly, so elastic that it will embrace anything, solemn, slight or beautiful that comes into my mind. I should like it to resemble some deep old desk, or capacious hold-all, in which one flings a mass of odds and ends without looking them through.
>
> Virginia Woolf, April 20, 1919

Some of you have already made your art into a career, and you have child-free waking hours scheduled into your routine. Others have only what you carve out of the inky night sky. But either way, long sanctified stretches, or short sporadic sprints, there will be times when the muse of inspiration chases hard and there's nothing you can do about it. Your hands are full of babies, schedules full of soccer games, life overflowing with family game nights, nights of sleep interrupted by growing pains and nightmares. You can't stop and answer the creative call that tugs at your heart, and so you set it aside, and you wait, and as you do you pray that the inspiration will be waiting for you too.

The day is coming when there is a bit more time to indulge your creative soul again, and when it arrives you will have journal upon journal of menus, decorating ideas, and lyrics all piled high. Until that time, perhaps you might ask yourself, "What sort of diary should I like mine to be?"

Chapter Six

Making Space

Making space to get really quiet and listen is
holy work.

Leeana Tankersley

Sometimes the sounds of life with all these precious people overwhelm me to the core. Not just babies crying and siblings argu-
ing, but the happy sounds too. All of it assailing my head and heart,
which long so much for silence. Silence like a blank canvas and the time
to fill it.

I'm like an overstimulated infant who needs the soothing rhythm of
a mother's rocking chair. Crying inwardly, and sometimes outwardly, I
look for that quiet place to rest. But art is my resting place, and I've no
time to crawl up into her lap and be at peace.

Artists are often sensitive people; easily moved, easily stimulated,
and easily undone. Maybe you know what I mean. We laugh the loud-
est and cry the hardest. We've traveled up to the magnificent heights yet
known the shadowy places of the valleys too. Sometimes it feels like a
curse, to feel as deeply and as constantly as we do, but indeed it is part
of the holy design. God made us to be deeply moved, that we might

move others deeply. Make no mistake: we were fashioned this way for a purpose, handcrafted sensitive, that we might tenderly communicate the beautiful and mysterious feelings of life.

During my junior year in college, my dad flew out to see me play the part of Julia in Thornton Wilder's *Our Town*. The themes of the play had touched my core and I gave each performance my best. The night my dad came to see the production, he met me backstage after the show, his eyes red-rimmed and watery. Because a handful of artists had done the hard work of being sensitive people, my dad, a man who doesn't talk much or communicate emotion easily, felt it and was moved to places he could not go alone. This is the gift we have been given, and the gift we give away.

Sensitive can be a painful place to live 24/7, though.

And so, in the years before marriage and children, I found a stable footing in the large sum of quiet that cradled me in my one-room apartment. I ate when I was hungry, slept long hours, and spent entire days writing with all the windows open. It was an artist's sanctuary, and in this safe haven I began to understand my tenderhearted hard wiring, and discovered the optimal, peaceful rhythm that allowed me to create. Then I became a wife and, shortly thereafter, a mother. And my quiet, coping space was filled with giggles and coos and sleepless nursing nights. At first it was divine. I thrived creatively, making hand-painted birth announcements and throwing my child's first party. But the quiet spaces that used to keep me grounded slowly shrank as my baby grew bigger.

> God made us to be deeply moved,
> that we might move others deeply.

Then came a sibling. Then another. And the quiet places of nap time grew busier as voices took to words. The thrill of those first words filled my days with an equal measure of delight and division. I was delighted and raptured by love but also divided from the white noise that used to give me peace, and my highly sensitive sensibilities turned on me. After the birth of my third child I even wrestled with feelings of anger. Agitated down deep in my core, I loved my children to the heavens, but my soul felt snared in the depths. And of course, there was the incessant guilt that made the chain heavier to bear. As my patience waned and my tears waxed I went to see my doctor. She suggested antidepressants.

Sweet, sensitive artists, depression is real. Sometimes it's chemical, where hormones lose their balance and adrenal glands get burned out, and we need medical attention. While I cannot diagnose a physical or emotional condition, I can encourage you to find holy places in your life where you can rest deeply, both literally and figuratively. When the unique needs of a sensitive soul go unmet day after day, year after year, there is the tendency to spiral downward into the pit.

> When the unique needs of a sensitive soul go unmet day after day, year after year, there is the tendency to spiral downward into the pit.

So grab your pen and underline anything in these pages ahead that offers hope, encouragement, and maybe some application too. Write in the margins to the left and to the right: "That! I can do that little bit; set that little bit of time aside, talk to the Lord about those dormant parts of myself, carve out moments and courage with the help of family and friends." Together we'll find time in your busy schedule around which to build hedges, like an artist's studio in your mind and in your days—a space and a place where you can steal away for some solitude, and there create.

Your Sanctification

I used to have a theory, highly scientific in nature, in which the children were conspiring to make me lose my mind. They were an organized bunch, working in perfect synchronicity so that the moment I had some quiet space it was filled in some way or another. All day long, and often through the night, I felt certain they had every moment mapped out. I could see them in my mind, putting their heads together when I had my back turned, sippy cups and bottles in front of them as they discussed their strategic battle plans for the days ahead. A well-oiled machine, they staggered diaper changes, temper tantrums, nightmares, and bedwetting in such a way that I could hardly sit down before another one needed me again.

On and on our days tumbled until I found myself grumbly and increasingly frustrated with this imagined conspiracy until I settled on anger, and I stewed there for a little while. It wasn't until a friend, a woman just on the other side of those years, pulled me aside and offered me some perspective that I finally escaped the clutches of this anger.

"You're upset with them for doing the one thing they cannot control," she told me over a cup of piping hot coffee. "They're just being children, and that's what children do."

Her words sank in, and immediately my spirit began to soften. The anger and frustration I felt toward my children were obviously misplaced, and really it was downright comical. And when I finally moved past the injustice of it all, I saw how this anger, rooted in selfishness, affected my children and my husband.

Here's an ugly truth: sensitive people can be incredibly insensitive when they lose themselves. I'd never been an angry woman until the quiet spaces of my life were threatened. Maybe you feel the same way, and I'm here to tell you that I understand. It seemed that all my fears—expressed so many years ago in our premarital counselor's office—had come true, and I was lost there in the chaos of all the needs. But in truth, I hadn't actually lost myself, but rather lost the space in which I could freely abide.

> Abide in Me, and I in you. As the branch cannot bear fruit of itself unless it abides in the vine, so neither can you unless you abide in Me. I am the vine, you are the branches; he who abides in Me and I in him, he bears much fruit, for apart from Me you can do nothing. (John 15:4–5)

More dangerous than a woman losing herself is the mom who's lost all semblance of God's fruit in her life. Because when a mom loses this fruit—love, joy, peace, patience, kindness, goodness, faithfulness, gentleness, and self-control—the entire home goes awry. So after my friend met with me, I called out fast and hard, "Lord, what's Your will for me? How do I do this mothering life, this sensitive creative

> More dangerous than a woman losing herself is the mom who's lost all semblance of God's fruit in her life.

life, this married faith life when it's all mashed up together without any breathing room? How do I do it all? What is Your will?"

What is Your will?

And there it is! The question we all come back to again and again over the course of our lives. What's Your will, God? It's neither a sensitive creative's question nor a mother's question; it is simply *the* question that humanity must repeatedly ask. And, praise God, there is an answer!

> For this is the will of God, your sanctification. (1 Thess. 4:3)

This one short verse tells us point blank what God's will is for us: *sanctification.* Your sanctification is God's utmost desire for the whole of your life. Every bit of it! The concrete parts of your mothering days, and those inspired, esoteric, dreamy corners too; all of it sanctified. So what is sanctification and how do we do it? How do we live it out in our hearts and homes, faith and family, during this season that's all mixed up together?

> **sanctification** (*noun*). The state of being set apart for the particular use intended by the designer; being set apart as holy or sacred.

Sanctification is the art of drawing away from this world in order to live transformed, Christlike lives. And this is God's will for you in every season of life: to be set apart in Him, for Him. And the greatest miracle of all is that your sanctification has already been done for you. "It is finished," Christ declared from the cross with his last breath. We have already been made holy by Jesus's sacrifice upon the cross. We were sinners, hell-bent and hardened, but the moment we believed and were saved, God pulled us from the muddy mess we'd made, cleaned us up, and set us apart on a firm foundation. Sanctified.

It's amazing, isn't it? The one thing God desires most for our lives, He already accomplished! And yet we get to partner with Him by living it out each day—continually working out our salvation! Living like it's true, making moment-by-moment choices that are in line with our set-apart reality.

> Only let us live up to what we have already attained. (Phil. 3:16 NIV)

Yes, we were made holy (when we put our faith in Christ), but we're also currently being made holy daily (as we keep in step with His Spirit). And when it's all said and done, on the other side of glory, we will be made completely holy as He is holy (when we stand before Him). So our sanctification is accomplished, and it is an active and ongoing process, and it's waiting for us too. What a mystery it is to know Christ!

And so we learn to sanctify each facet of our beautiful, complicated days. Believing all of it to be *sanctified*—set apart as holy. Practically speaking, we must find ways each day to pull away and say, "This is my sanctified time with the Lord—I set it apart as holy. This is my sanctified time with my family—I set it apart as holy. This is my sanctified time in the workforce—I set it apart as holy. This is my sanctified time to create—I set it apart as holy too." Child of God, homemaker, working mom, artist—every bit of you set apart for Him.

> Child of God, homemaker, working mom, artist—every bit of you set apart for Him.

Sanctified Time with God

Susanna Wesley was a woman well acquainted with challenge. Married to Sam Wesley, a preacher who was gone for long stretches of time, she spent many nights alone, and management of their busy household fell solely on her shoulders. In addition to juggling their constant debt, Susanna birthed nineteen children, ten of whom survived. One of her children was crippled, another didn't walk until nearly six years old, and Susanna herself was often ill. Their family home burned to the ground on two different occasions, and at times there wasn't enough money for food.

And yet, in the midst of this chaos, as Susanna took care of their home and milked their cow and schooled the children, she mastered this art of pulling away, daily retreating to spend time in prayer with her Lord. But where, you might wonder, could she go to find a solitary place? Since solitude wasn't an option, Susanna decided that her time in worship and prayer would be found under her apron. She let her children know that when her apron was lifted up over her head, she was not to be disturbed. That was her sanctified time.

What an example for us. The sanctified time of a mother, pulling away in the midst of so many responsibilities. Can you imagine the fruit that would spring up from such abiding in your home? Starting, of course, with the fruit of peace, patience, and love growing up out of the fertile soil of the heart that beats behind your own metaphoric apron.

> Very early in the morning, while it was still dark, Jesus got up,
> left the house and went off to a solitary place, where he prayed.
> (Mark 1:35 NIV)

Absolutely, part of a healthy, sanctified, spiritual life is spent in prayer, talking to the One who already accomplished our sanctification. But Jesus then calls us deeper, showing us how to continue the process.

> Sanctify them in the truth; Your word is truth. (John 17:17)

If you find yourself wobbling emotionally in this overwhelming season of motherhood, let me encourage you again to set apart time each and every day to meet God in His living Word. This does, of course, feel entirely impossible with only a few hours of sleep, and with cease-less hours shuttling, serving, and loving. But it is paramount that we pursue this ongoing, transformative relationship with our Savior daily in the truth of His Word. Like Susanna Wesley tucked beneath her apron, we must pull away, telling the children that now is the time Mom meets with her Lord. The implications of this discipline will go far beyond our own sanctified hearts as our children watch and learn, and grow in the knowledge of a set-apart life.

Two of the Wesley children, Charles and John, grew up to be credited with bringing spiritual revival to England. Charles is known to be one of the greatest hymn writers in history, penning such masterful works of praise and adoration as "Hark! The Herald Angels Sing," "Christ the Lord Is Risen Today," and "Come Thou Long Expected Jesus"; and John was a theologian who still influences discourse in today's church. There is no denying that a mother's sanctified life carries great influence.

So what might this look like in your home, amidst your busy mothering days? First thing in the morning? In the parking lot after dropping your children off at school? At night, on the couch, as they drift off to sleep down the hall? There's no formula for abiding, only the promise that *when* we do abide in Him, He abides in us—His peace, His patience, His joy and love, His gentleness, faithfulness and self-control.

As we serve our loved ones each livelong day, let us remember Jesus's friends, the sisters Mary and Martha who represent us all. The one who served strenuously until she was weary and worn, dear Martha is the reality of our long disjointed days. Days where we are distracted and worried and upset about many things. In contrast to Mary, who sat at her Savior's feet, soaking up His nearness, of whom Christ said, "Mary has chosen what is better" (Luke 10:42 NIV).

Sanctified Time with Family

To us, family means putting your arms around each other and being there.

Barbara Bush

Being there is hard. Oh, I know that you're always *there*, just as Martha was always serving, but sanctifying family time is one of the biggest challenges for moms today. One moment, one need, one meal, one bath, one more lullaby—all tumble ceaselessly together. In the mad dash of motherhood it's easy to forget to slow down and wrap your arms around the season, around your people.

Sanctifying family time requires that we stop and purposefully participate in the holy celebration of unity. And do you see that there are two parts to that equation? First, we learn to *stop,* and then we intentionally *do* something.

It was 1998, and I was living in Kiev, Ukraine. Long days of trying to understand and speak a foreign language often left me fatigued, my head a jumbled mess of Russian grammar. My favorite place to escape to during those months was the *Pechersk Lavra*, a centuries-old monastery still in operation. I'd walk past the cobbled walls, rebuilt after the bombings of World War II, and a hush would fall over my soul. I spent hours wandering the grounds of that hallowed space, traversing beneath the earth to the catacombs, the chilled air tickling my arms as the silence hummed loudly, chasing away all the chaotic noise of the outside world. There was peace inside those walls, because everything else had been left outside the wooden gates.

And so it is for sanctified, hallowed moments with family. One of the greatest challenges of having a creative hobby or a creative home business is learning to build these invisible walls around our time together. It's imperative we do. The inspiration is always present, and our desk is just down the hall . . . but so is our spouse, and so are our children. So we commit to fortifying ourselves, holding the outside world at arm's length. Again we need application: How might this look? Perhaps it's unplugging from all technology during mealtimes, or shutting off all online communication during the weekends. Things like setting a predictable schedule or making family dinnertime a priority will provide sacred, sanctified time for families.

And let us not forget the power of traditions! Saturday morning pancake feasts and Sunday afternoon hikes through the nearby hills are a surefire way to connect with one another. Establishing traditions is a proactive way to say, "Family is a priority in my life. I've made the time, scheduled it, set it apart as holy . . ." Habits keep the sanctifying process moving forward from day to day, week to week, season after season— together with your family, together with the Lord, together with your creative self.

Sanctified Time to Create

The eldest is lean and long like his father, standing at the sink, scrubbing breakfast dishes while his two youngest brothers are still at the table. Their mother has the other three boys, helping them get ready for a school day. Altogether there are six sons asking about missing socks, needing help to hang towels properly, and clamoring for attention. Though she homeschools her children three days a week, the other two days they head to a private school where their father is the headmaster. Those are the days she works.

> Sometimes we're called to lay down the art to focus entirely on *the art of mothering.*

Ruth Simons is the artist behind Gracelaced.com, painting and writing her way through long mothering days. For the first thirteen years of her life as *Mom*, Ruth chose purposefully to set aside her palette of paint, because sometimes we're called to lay down the art to focus entirely on *the art of mothering.*

When she did eventually pick up her brush again and then open wide the laptop, she did so carefully, with boundaries and caution. At first it was simply nap times, or with a child upon her knee, but as her online business grew, and eventually exploded, Ruth started painting in the evenings as well. And when the workload grew so heavy that it encroached upon sacred family time, Ruth hired help. Not much, but enough.

Today it takes a small team to help her run her creative ministry, with a personal assistant, one sweet mother's helper, and a troupe of interns

helping to manage the constant flow of orders. Friday is Ruth's sanctified workday—one full day to get all the business errands done. Often
times, when she returns from an afternoon of meetings and writing,
she finds her children all in the GraceLaced Shoppe together, sleeving
prints and stamping envelopes.

Jim Elliot was famous for saying, "Wherever you are, be all there."
With the help of her small team, Ruth humbly attempts this sanctified,
all-there life each day. Still actively present shaping young minds, molding play dough, and planning the many meals it takes to feed a pack
of growing man-cubs. Purposing other sanctified moments to work on
blog posts, participating in design consultations and conference calls,
and putting brush to canvas, finding solace in the place where it all
began—her art. She's found a rhythm in her sanctified life—a time for
art, a time for business, and always time for family. There is order—or
at least as much order as one can have while raising six boys—in each
carefully planned day.

Life is, of course, not void of chaos or stress in the Simons household.
There are still scheduling conflicts, hurt feelings, and miscommunica-
tion, as there will be in any family. But even when it all crashes together
in disorder, Ruth uses the chaos to demonstrate grace to her loved ones.
Yes, even the disorder becomes an opportunity for sanctification.

Order and boundary lines keep us safe, offering freedom in each
carefully chosen moment. The hope is, of course, when we operate
from this place of sanctified structure, we can in turn give our children the best parts of us, including great gobs of time loving and feeding and playing with them. With time set aside purposefully with the
Lord, we ensure that our spirits also do not shrivel in this season of life.
And the sensitive, quiet soul that needs to pull away and create can rest
assured that there will be time for that too. Sanctified time set apart
as holy, because it is. All of it. And so are you. Holy and dearly loved.

This idea of setting boundaries around your time with the Lord isn't
new, and being intentional in your mothering isn't a fresh idea either.
But pair those two things together with this idea of consecrated creative

time, and now we're talking about our whole flourishing, multifaceted lives. With these three areas continually refined, we begin to find order in our consecrated, sanctified, fruit-bearing lives. And it is here that an overwhelmed soul finds rest.

Chapter Seven

Renaissance Worship

. . . life and art are never about applause—and always about altars.

Ann Voskamp

When the cries pierced my dreams, I jolted awake. The monitor by my side once again gave the jarring call that pulled me from the warmth of my bed, and I sighed impatiently. She had been sleeping through the night for months, but a growth spurt now caused her to demand more of me multiple times a night, and on this fourth midnight in a row I found myself exhausted and near tears.

I stumbled to her room shaking the bottle, eyes heavy with fatigue. Picking her up out of bed, I pulled her close and kissed her warm, doughy cheek, which did little to abate my intense longing for bed. We settled into the rocking chair, and as she ate, I closed my eyes and tried to doze, but instead the words floated through my head, and I couldn't help but look down at her as I ingested the poem I'd read long ago.

> Little Lamb who made thee
> Dost thou know who made thee

Gave thee life & bid thee feed.
By the stream & o'er the mead;
Gave thee clothing of delight,
Softest clothing wooly bright;
Gave thee such a tender voice,
Making all the vales rejoice!
    Little Lamb who made thee
    Dost thou know who made thee
              William Blake
              Songs of Inncoence, 1789

I whispered these words, and her eyes drifted shut while my own filled with tears. Filled to overflowing with humble, grateful praise for the privilege and opportunity to hold this perfect, tiny being in my arms. That moment in my big yellow rocker was one of worship. It was my exhausted, poured-out, spiritual service of worship to God.

Therefore I urge you, brethren, by the mercies of God, to present your bodies a living and holy sacrifice, acceptable to God, which is your spiritual service of worship. (Rom. 12:1)

While our artistic offerings are, no doubt, beautiful acts of worship, they are not our only offerings. Remember, Renaissance moms are skilled and gifted in diverse ways. The work you do on a canvas or on a stage is part of your worshipful life as a living sacrifice; however, it is the parts that seem mundane and unseen in our *ordinary days* that have the potential to become our most fragrant offerings. We must, therefore, step back and look at the whole tapestry of each day to truly understand the totality of a Renaissance mom's worship. She bakes, she sews, she sings . . . she cleans, she cooks, she tickles backs, she potty trains, she prays for her loved ones, she befriends her neighbors . . . and all of it she does with sincerity of heart, as unto the Lord.

worship (*noun*). The act of offering extravagant admiration, esteem, honor, reverence, devotion, love, and respect to God.

From dawn to dusk and through the night, the myriad ways that a mother worships are boundless. Which is why we often peter out, and lose track of the artistic parts of our worshipful lives. But all of it, *all of it,* is worship. Renaissance worship.

For this reason I remind you to kindle afresh the gift of God which is in you through the laying on of my hands. (2 Tim. 1:6)

When Wanida leads worship, the room around her ignites, charged by the unbridled passion that flows through her every movement. Hands raised, face lifted high, cheeks flushed—she's all in, and her art is music, and those who worship with her are led deep into the presence of God. They're led by the Spirit, that's true, but He uses a woman, a *mother*, to fan the flames. Beyond her obvious talent, Wanida displays an authentic joy and deep faith that ignites everyone around her. As her fingers dance atop the black and white keys, her entire countenance changes to one of joy.

Wanida's creative gift goes beyond vocals and the piano. She plays an array of instruments, moving from one to the next until she finally settles on the drums. With her band backing her up, she lifts the drumsticks high over her head and pounds, and the rhythm matches your heartbeat, or maybe it's the other way around, until it's all jumbled together, and she's laughing, and you're clapping. And everyone is part of the offering. Delighted worship lifted high. Art cased in flesh, beat on a silver drum.

When the song is finished she exits the stage, hands shaking because joy will do that to you, and she's greeted at the bottom of the stairs by two of her girls. They bounce and wiggle, and clap their hands because mom just moved a mountain through song.

The worship leader is now all mom as she walks them back to their seats, art and life all mashed up. Her sacrificial worship on the stage now becomes the sacrificial act of motherhood as she sits with her children and gently hushes them so that they hear the message of Jesus come to this earth as a baby. Her eyes water at the story, at the curly-haired moppets by her side, at the longing to point them to Him.

Wanida's life, the masterpiece that it is, is one giant act of worship, each day offered as a gift back to the Giver. Mom, wife, musician—it's all an offering, giving away and pouring out oneself. This is the living, breathing picture of worship.

It's All Worship

As the passing of time brings about fine lines around my eyes and the surprising appearance of gray hair at my temples, I'm aware that other things are changing too. Wisdom and perspective are making their home inside my bones as the years roll on. I'm thankful for this spiritual stretching as it makes the process of growing older a lovely thing indeed. Looking back from where I stand today, I see that all these years have been one interwoven thread of worship: *avodah.*

> Worship isn't just something we do at church with heads bowed. Worship is a chin-up, face-forward thing too.

Avodah is a solitary word with three diverse meanings braided together in real life: work, worship, and service. This one ancient Hebrew word has helped shape my understanding of what it means for a woman to worship every day of the week, everywhere I go, because worship isn't just something we do at church with heads bowed. Worship is a chin-up, face-forward thing too. It happens at home, and at work, and at church. It's the voice, hand, and foot service of my day-to-day life.

Avodah.

As multitaskers, women are known to have a slew of activity around them at all times, all of it swirling together, every moment of every day. Our mothering, serving, ministry, working, married lives flow together like a seamless, albeit dizzying, dance. It bleeds together without start or stop. Worship, work, and service fill each moment of our days, each room and relationship, every corner of the home. And all of our lives grow up and out of this one root system—one root word.

Avodah.

In Exodus 8:1, Moses demands that Pharaoh let the Israelites leave Egypt, so that they might go and worship Him in the desert. "This is what the LORD says: Let my people go, so that they may worship [*avodah*] me" (NIV). This was the command for all God's people to worship Him collectively, and this is our call to church community as well—worshipping and fellowshipping, tithing and serving, taking Communion together as we lift up and worship the name of Jesus.

Avodah.

However, later in Exodus 34:21, Moses uses the word again. Moses, renewing the covenant with God, says, "Six days you shall labor [*avodah*]" (NIV). This same word exhorts us to worship the Lord with our muscles and our minds the rest of the week as we toil. And then Joshua (Moses's young assistant) takes the word and its meaning a step further when he proclaims, "But as for me and my household, we will serve [*avodah*] the LORD" (Josh. 24:15 NIV). With one bold proclamation, the scope of this act of worship is widened exponentially.

Avodah.

Of the 261 verses where this word appears in the Bible, the translations include everything from working and laboring, to worship services and ceremonies, to serving the Lord together as a family from one's home. Don't all these words whisper of a mother's full life? Aren't they all one in the same? And yet we keep trying to define each part as something uniquely separate.

Grace for the Hard Days

From the moment you pull yourself out of bed until your head hits the pillow again, you're met with countless opportunities to worship. It isn't confined to the few songs you help lead on Sunday morning, but is, instead, *all* the moments of your everyday consecrated life.

It seems as though this should be easy, doesn't it? The head knowledge that all of life is sacred worship is simple enough to grasp intellectually. But in the moments when the children are screaming and dinner is burning, and your husband calls to tell you he'll be late, you may find yourself feeling less than worshipful, and more longing to just escape for a few minutes . . . or days. Realistically, you and I both know that seeing each moment of the day as worship is incredibly difficult. We simply won't always feel like that, and here's what I want you to know: *it's okay.*

A Renaissance man was never known to be automatically gifted in all of his pursuits, but rather dedicated to studying and increasing in each individual area of expertise. Likewise, we understand that our first screenplay most likely won't win an Oscar, our first quilt may not receive the blue ribbon at the fair. We may not receive top honors with our first literary offering, and our first paintings may be rudimentary at best. We've got *learning* to do.

> From the moment you pull yourself out of bed until your head hits the pillow again, you're met with countless opportunities to worship.

The same is true in our home lives. As Renaissance moms, we want to get better in all our skills as craftspeople, mothers, wives, and worshippers. And we must also grow in our ability to extend grace to our hearts when we fail. By recognizing and acknowledging that not every poured-out moment will be met with success (or a joyful heart), we allow ourselves the freedom to be refined by God even when it's hard. Especially when it's hard.

You are learning to be a mother, and each new phase of your children's development brings new challenges. Just when you think you've got it figured out, they enter a new phase, and you start the process all over again.

You're learning to be a wife. Parenting growing children alongside your spouse brings new challenges to a marriage. Along with career changes, promotions, layoffs, the illness or death of aging parents, and a whole host of other life issues, you get to continually practice the fine art of living and serving others.

You are also forever learning to be an artisan. As your art moves with you in and out of different seasons, it naturally changes. Together you grow—the art and the artist—as you master your skill set, comprehending the message you want your art to convey. There is always so much work to be done.

And ultimately, you are always, forever learning to be a Christ-follower. Through every challenge, every change, and every trial, in every joy and every jubilee, you are growing up and into a clearer reflection of our Savior. Always so much learning.

But there's more to this worshipful equation, for the enemy is present and active, and always on the prowl, ready and waiting to yank the worship out from beneath our feet. And here it is that we dig deeper into God's grace.

Humble Offerings

I sat on the couch, blinking against the tears that threatened to spill onto my cheeks. My husband sat beside me, gently rubbing my arm as I tried to process my swirling emotions. We were new in town and this would be my first Sunday helping to lead worship at our new church. I had been through this before, but thought I had moved past that awkward place where worship and performance compete. But God was still growing me in this regard.

"I just don't know how," I confessed it aloud. "I'm afraid to really let go up there, because then it looks like it's all about me! I don't want it to be about me."

When I was small, I found great pleasure and confidence onstage with a microphone. I didn't really consider this gift an act of worship until I went to college. Up until then, singing was for my own satisfaction. It was simply performance, and I was good at it. I liked the praise I received, and the adrenaline I felt after entertaining a crowd. It wasn't until later on, when I learned to understand performance and worship in a healthy way, that I began to see my gift as an offering to His glory, not my own. But this understanding opened up an entirely different struggle.

I grew paralyzed with fear before every song, certain that I would be seen as a fraud, frivolously begging for adulation, because the truth is sometimes the music takes over, and the notes come out strong and full, and people are moved. I see it and feel it. But there's a nagging voice in my head that questions if they think I'm just putting on a show. Desperately longing to lead people to a place of worship, I feared becoming a distraction, so I pulled back and slunk into the shadows, underutilizing my God-given gift.

But my husband knows me better, because he knows my heart. He leaned in close that day and looked at me with a gentle smile. "You have a unique gift," he told me, his voice warm and reassuring. My heart slowed as I listened to his wisdom. "When you sing, and I mean *really* sing, you have this ability to lead people into a place of true worship. You aren't showing off because it's not about you. It's about Him. I know that, and so do you. It's time to stop worrying what others might think about *you*, and simply let go and worship with the voice God gave you. Because—when you do that—that's when the rest of us come along."

Pride is a wily beast, rooted in the innate self-love of our sinful nature. Sneaking in when we least expect it, pride siphons off our ability to worship God by turning the focus of our days inward. Pride whispers lovely thoughts into our ears, dictating how we operate both in the privacy of home and in full view under the spotlights. Pride distorts it all, and it quickly gets so twisted. Before long, we've convinced ourselves that we're making better choices for our children and our marriages and God's fame, when all we're really after is our own glorification. How sly the devil is.

For creatives who live out a part of this worshipful life on a public stage, the temptation to fall into pride is naturally stronger. We find delight in the expression of our particular talents, and a measure of glee when we stumble upon successes, come in contact with people we believe to be important, or step into a coveted place of leadership. Christian popularity and ministry fame is a slippery slope. It happens fast, and often we don't even realize we've fallen prey. So we must remain ever vigilant, always at the ready to combat thinking more highly of ourselves than we ought. But there's a flip side to this prideful coin, for waiting in the wings just off-stage is pride's ever present and equally destructive companion, insecurity, often masked in false humility.

> Sneaking in when we least expect it, pride siphons off our ability to worship God by turning the focus of our days inward.

Artistic talents, particularly those in the performing arts, garner such visceral praise from those around us. People are moved by worship, by performance, by music and drama, and by a well-delivered talk. Quick to flee from a prideful response, we can run, well intentioned, to the other extreme. There we begin to believe that we really have no skill at all, as though somehow we just stumbled into these artistic capabilities quite by accident, leaving the stage awkwardly with an embarrassed wave.

True humility is the opposite of pride. Humility is not, however, self-deprecation, for it was never meant to be the result of a low opinion of ourselves. We must recognize each humble offering for what it truly is— the talents that we have stewarded well! From there we are able to move on without thinking either too highly of ourselves *or* too lowly of God's gifts. From that place, Satan loses all power to thwart our worship.

Consider the following passage from C. S. Lewis's *The Screwtape Letters* in which the demon, Screwtape, is writing to his nephew, Wormwood. His sole purpose is to help Wormwood tempt the man placed in his charge.

> You must therefore conceal from the patient the true end of Humility. Let him think of it not as self-forgetfulness but as a certain kind of opinion (namely, a low opinion) of his own

talents and character. . . . Fix in his mind the idea that humility consists in trying to believe those talents to be less valuable than he believes them to be. . . . The Enemy [God] wants to bring the man to a state of mind in which he could design the best cathedral in the world, and know it to be the best, and rejoice in the fact, without being any more (or less) or otherwise glad at having done it than he would be if it had been done by another.

Your creative gift, dear mom, is a recognizable one. What you do with a lump of dough, with the canvas of a blank computer screen or the instrument in your hands, holds weight in this world that longs for beauty. Praise will come, be sure of that, but decide in your heart beforehand what you'll do with the attention. The temptation will either be to accept the praise for yourself or, conversely, to refuse any sort of praise at all. Neither of these responses glorifies the Gift Giver, and both hinder worship. There have been times in the past when I've tried to compliment someone for the impact her art had on me, only to have her brush off my praise without making eye contact, speaking in a rote response, "Oh, it's all the Lord. He gets all the praise."

This is inevitably followed by an awkward silence.

This may feel like the right and "humble" response, but as Lewis's admonition in *The Screwtape Letters* so eloquently points out, that isn't actually humility, but rather misdirected pride. Of course it is true: the Lord *does* get all the praise, because every good and perfect gift has come from Him. But it's okay to also acknowledge your part in the offering. You presented it, worked at it for hours on end as an act of worship. Don't shy away from the generous applause of appreciation by recipients of your art.

It's complicated, I know, but when you embrace your talent for what

> Praise will come, be sure of that, but decide in your heart beforehand what you'll do with the attention.

it is—a gift from God that you've given back to Him—you are worshipping. Know it in your heart! But also know that your offering intimately affects others, often leading them to a uniquely worshipful place as well. Thank them for their compliments, and tell them how much it means to you to hear how the Lord is ministering to them through the time of worship together—or through the painting, the poem, the dramatic monologue, the way you throw a party . . .

One of the things I most admire about my friend Wanida's brand of worship is the way she embraces her skills. Watching Wanida worship moves everyone around her to worship because she simply gives in to the musical praise. It is the thing that was placed before her, this musical gifting, and she lives it fully and completely, all to the glory of the One to whom she sings.

> Shout for joy to the LORD, all the earth.
>   Worship the LORD with gladness;
>   come before him with joyful songs.
> Know that the LORD is God. (Ps. 100:1–3 NIV)

God has placed before you a responsibility unlike any other as you train up the small people in your midst. When they're young, they won't recognize each meal and book and trip to the park as an act of worship. They may see it as nothing more than your duty. After all, you're "Mom." It's your job to feed them and cart them around, right? But we know that this is so much more than a job. These mothering moments are consecrated acts of worship, presented to the Lord with the same heart that beats behind your Sunday dress as you belt out a solo or teach the story of David and Goliath to a roomful of five-year-olds. By acknowledging the tasks that He places before you, and faithfully attending to each one, you live life worshipfully.

When you drag yourself from the warm cocoon of your bed sheets to feed a crying baby, this is your spiritual service of worship.

When you stoop low and fill in her rainbow with crayons, a tow-headed toddler sitting by your side, this is your spiritual service of worship.

When you wake up early and sit at the keyboard, pulling the headphones over your ears so you can play freely without disturbing your slumbering household, this is your spiritual service of worship.

Putting money in the offering plate, rocking babies in the nursery, sprinkling glitter over handprints in the preschool room, all of it your spiritual service of worship.

Those cakes you spent the afternoon making so that you can celebrate a fanciful seven-year-old's birthday? That was worship too.

Leading your children in morning devotions before driving them to school. Worship.

Cleaning dirty floors, painting empty canvases, folding loads of laundry, penning lyrics to the music that swirls in your head—worshipping, working, serving, laboring . . . All of this is sacred Renaissance worship.

Avodah.

Chapter Eight

The Art of Home

Ah! there is nothing like staying at home for
real comfort.

Jane Austen, Emma

She flits about the house, gathering items from each room, piling them in the center of the foyer. When she's certain she's pulled all that she can, she loads as many things into her arms as possible, kicks open the door, and treads across the yard to the waiting barn. Back and forth she goes until she's hauled it all, her husband watching with a bemused smile, because he's seen that look in her eye before. He knows that the creativity is rushing over her like a wave, and he can't help but feel excitement for what waits on the other side of her inspiration.

For Myquillyn Smith, better known to most of the online world as The Nester, home is her inspiration. It is her ministry, her comfort, and the place where all her loved ones gather close and love deeply. Home has also become Myquillyn's business. From her booming website, The Nesting Place, she encourages women to find the beauty already residing inside the walls of their home. And by her side is the calming presence of her husband, Chad.

Chad and Myquillyn have lived their lives boldly through her blog, sharing inspirational stories about their family life, learning to be content with less, paying off debt through hard work and sacrifice, and building a business. Then they brought their online community into the circle of their new dreams. They dreamed of a new place that could become more than just home, of a larger gathering place to build and deepen community. When they discovered property in the hills of North Carolina, they knew it was meant for them—the most compelling reason being the large, metal tractor barn that begged to be redone in The Nester's cheery signature style.

Turning the barn into a gathering place took a little sweat equity as Chad and friends worked furiously to make it the perfect home for their real-life events. When it was move-in ready, Myquillyn took over, furnishing the space almost completely with possessions she already owned. Her artistic vision for decorating on a budget transformed the white walls into a beautiful, inviting space for people to connect. She placed the vase with the deep crack down the back in the corner, and filled it with dried eucalyptus from the roadside. Draping a beaded necklace over the antlers hung on the wall, she stepped back and took it all in. Reaching for her camera, she climbed a ladder to photograph the space meant to share with her family and community. And when the camera's shutter snapped, she captured home.

She captured art.

Back in the early pages of this book we purposed to begin this Renaissance movement from the confines of our own holy Jerusalem, within the border of our homes. From there we asked God's Spirit to lead us forth into the neighboring towns of Judea and Samaria, serving in our local communities as opportunity and time permitted in our mothering days. Slivers grew into larger segments of time as children moved into school years, and family and friends partnered with us, giving room to create. Then we spoke the words, "Here am I, send me," and God gave us vision to use our creativity for His glory out in the world.

Many of you have literally gone to the far corners of the Earth with your creative giftedness, taking pictures of orphans in developing world nations, raising awareness and funds, visiting missionaries and writing their stories as they love on the poorest of the poor. However, there are others of you who feel called very specifically to focus all your energy and talent on the ministry within your own four walls. Not only the precious ministry to your children, but the brick and mortar, the plaster and paint, the carpet and blinds. Home is your inspiration and it's all the art you've ever dreamed of. Decorating, child-rearing, and menu planning fill you up to overflowing, so you create from that running-over place. Home for some is not only where everything begins, it *is* everything. For many a woman, home is her magnum opus.

> For many a woman, home is her magnum opus.

In this grand Renaissance procession, women are leading the way— expressing themselves boldly from their kitchens, living rooms, and home offices, and serving their families with more creativity and flare than ever before. The amazing thing is that all this living and loving is not necessarily confined to the home anymore. With the various channels available on the Internet, the impact can reach across borders and lands. As simple as it sounds, these women are teaching us a thing or two about hospitality in the way they adorn their tables with flowers from the garden, make homemade board games for their children, and host dinner parties for work colleagues, family, and friends.

> **hospitality** (*noun*). Gracious friendship and welcoming generosity extended to those who enter one's home; the provision of refreshment, comfort, ease, and pleasure to guests or travelers.

Indeed, homemaking is at the very core of this creative movement, because for some women home is the art. Their creativity is entirely satisfied with the subject matter at their fingertips.

For some creative women . . .
Home is their content and their context.
Home is their subject and their setting.
Home is their mission and their message.
Home is their work and their worship.

Inspired at Home

In January 2006, Melissa Michaels sensed the Lord calling her to serve Him in some radical new way beyond her home life. Days turned into weeks turned into months of asking, "Why me? I'm happy here. How?" But the answers didn't come. She was sure that serving Him outside of their home would require physically leaving her comfortable place and sacrificing everything she was already doing and so desperately loved. Confused, because she didn't feel talented or equipped to serve in ways beyond her love for family and faith, and the home that encapsulated both, Melissa sought diligently for wisdom.

After months of searching and questioning, she came to the place where she opened her hands and her home and gave it all up to Him, a living sacrifice so to speak. "God, you can have it," she whispered. "Every bit. You can have my dreams, my comfort, my abilities, and my inabilities. You tell me what to do and I will say *Yes*. Here I am. Use me however You wish."

The next morning came early and the sky was clear as she walked through empty hallways to her home office, and in the supernatural way that only the Holy Spirit can speak, Melissa felt God give everything she was willing to sacrifice right back to her. Rather like Abraham and Isaac, God brought a simple homemaker to the altar place where she laid it tearfully and faithfully down, only to have it redeemed and rewarded. Melissa was inspired by the Lord to begin an exciting new ministry right where she was, there in the confines of the home she loved so much.

That very morning, Melissa responded to the Holy Spirit's prompting by turning on the computer and starting her blog, *The Inspired Room*. Home became the connection point with other women all around the world. When she hit publish for the first time, she imagined a small circle of readers from her church and community. She never fathomed that the work, the worship, and the service of a simple, creative homemaker could have such fruitful results, resonating with scores of women internationally. So many that in both 2014 and 2015, *The Inspired Room* was voted reader's favorite decorating blog by *Better Homes and Gardens*.

Not only does Melissa weekly inspire women to enjoy the home they have, she uses every opportunity to point her readers to the God who provides their every need and loves them desperately! And every time she feels like pulling back from her gospel-centered posts, she remembers the Holy Spirit's faithful whisper on the day she began blogging: "*The harvest is great but the workers are few.*"

Older women likewise are to be reverent in their behavior, not malicious gossips nor enslaved to much wine, teaching what is good, so that they may encourage the young women to love their husbands, to love their children, to be sensible, pure, workers at home, kind, being subject to their own husbands, so that the word of God will not be dishonored. (Titus 2:3–5)

Something remarkable has happened in this digital generation: mentors, as described in Titus 2, are now flourishing in our virtual midst. Funny thing is, many of them aren't much older than we are. In fact, some of these mentors are practically our peers—women like September McCarthy, who may have a couple years of growth and learning on new moms but is still deep in the trenches herself, raising ten children in the rural hills of upstate New York.

While her lap is often full of little people, and the countertops hold a menagerie of bottled bugs and frogs in cardboard boxes, September isn't content to hoard her wisdom for herself, but rather extends it outward like a lifeline. Uniquely attuned to the needs of hurting women, she is quick to invite readers to journey along with her to the high places of hope and healing.

Having traversed the heartbreaking road of miscarriage four times along with three full-term infant losses, September understands the deep aching places, and she longs to point others toward God's tender love in the midst of it all. She is also passionate about raising up the next generation to know and love that same faithful Father. With all this in mind, September founded an annual national conference, aptly named *Raising Generations Today*. Gathering writers and speakers to minister to moms face-to-face, these creative communicators encourage younger women "to love their husbands, to love their children, to be sensible, pure, workers at *home*, kind, being subject to their own husbands, so that the word of God will not be dishonored" (Titus 2:4–5).

Of course, one mom with ten children cannot possibly pour into hundreds of others on a daily basis. And so September uses social media as a means to reach out to the world. This is the faithful pouring out of a Titus 2 woman living boldly in this digital age.

But homebound writers aren't the only ones encouraging women today. Christian artisans are making jewelry, baking pies, and sharing their estate sale finds—all the while using their social media platforms "to teach what is good."

Visual artist Melissa Lyons started painting in 2012, shortly after becoming a mom. Painting hadn't been part of her life plan, until the day she heard the Lord tell her to pick up a brush. It was a quick and natural launch. She put a few early pieces on Etsy and opened up an Instagram account, and hasn't ever looked back. Eventually she also started a website where she blogs about her life, her faith, and her latest work of art. One of those webpages is titled "Our Testimony." This is the place where she bares more than her creativity; it's the page where she writes out the long and sin-stained life that Jesus saved Melissa and her husband from. She is raw and blunt and fiercely committed to sharing the good news of forgiveness through faith in Christ.

While I was originally drawn to her acrylics, I now eagerly anticipate her words. She's not my elder; in fact, her children are younger than mine, so she's likely younger than me too! But still she models for me these Titus 2 virtues as she daily fights to live them out. From her home she comes like a faithful friend into mine. Never having to leave her family life—where she parents and paints and preaches mini sermons on Instagram.

A mere decade ago we were confined alone to our homes, and walked around our churches wondering where to find a mentor, but today they abound in the virtual church. Women are leading by example, not just through their art, but also from their lives . . . at home.

> A mere decade ago we were confined alone to our homes, and walked around our churches wondering where to find a mentor, but today they abound in the virtual church.

There is a danger, however, as we peer into their Pinterest-worthy websites and compare their homes to ours. A feeling of inadequacy can quickly and easily set in, nagging at our senses until we've become quite discontent in the real life spaces that surround us.

The Threat of Discontent

In 2013, my husband and I brought a young woman into our home through an orphan-hosting program. She was a teenager from Eastern Europe who had spent her formative years in an orphanage without the loving guidance of a mother or father to teach her even the basics of everyday life.

We immediately fell in love with this gentlehearted individual, despite the challenges she brought with her. Because of her age and situation, we were unable to adopt her, so she lives permanently across the ocean, and our parenting takes place via email, sporadic phone calls, and care packages.

I periodically send her boxes filled with things I know she needs, and a few items I know she wants. She's nineteen now, trying to live independently in a land that sees her as second class. As the demands of life begin to weigh her down, I try to lift her up with my words and tangible displays of loving care, but sometimes my love and gifts aren't received the way I'd like them to be. A few months after her last visit, I sent her a box of clothes and magazines, and tucked forty dollars into the pocket of her new jeans to help her pay for schoolbooks.

Two weeks later I received an email. It was one single, solitary line that cut me to the core and tore into my mother's heart. "Mama. You only sent $40. Why didn't you send $50?" There was no thank you, no gratitude to show me she appreciated my gesture. There was simply a demand for more, and it hurt me.

Later that day, I opened up Instagram and skimmed through my feed, taking in the joy-filled smiles of color-coordinated children, clean countertops, and healthy plates of fresh fruit and vegetables. And then I happened upon an online acquaintance announcing that she was writing another book. For years I had been trying to get my first book published to no avail, and it seemed I was daily accosted with others who were walking the path of what I believed to be *my* dream. As if I somehow owned the rights to that particular vision.

As I moved throughout my evening, cleaning up messes, wiping noses, breaking up arguments, I felt myself increasingly frustrated with what I believed to be my unfair lot in life. My home wasn't sun-drenched or Pinterest-worthy, and *she* was writing books while I was changing diapers. I let this sinful thought pattern simmer until it boiled over in heated tears. Falling into my oversized yellow chair, I leaned my head back and looked up, hoping somehow that the Lord would write a promise in the air above my head that my time was coming.

Instead, my seven-year-old climbed out of his bed and made his way into my lap. He'd been running a fever all day and simply needed his mom to hold him, to tell him it was going to be okay. And maybe that was the answer to my own feverish heartache over wishing for more, for different, for cleaner, better, brighter. Maybe the cuddles of a sick little boy were what it took for the Lord to gently lead me away from what I felt was lacking, and toward the full-bodied reality of where He'd placed me. My life was mine not by *accident*, but by God's design. His story for me was unique, and it fit only me.

Once I had him nestled into bed again, I made my way back to the comfort of that chair and pulled out my Bible. I was desperate for refreshment after a long day of disappointment.

> Or do you think lightly of the riches of His kindness and tolerance and patience, not knowing that the kindness of God leads you to repentance? (Rom. 2:4)

I read this verse and was immediately seized with conviction as I thought of the teenage girl on the other side of the world who seemed so ungrateful for the gift I'd sent. As my mind drifted back to the pictures of other families in other homes, other countertops overflowing with other meals, and then to my response at another woman's celebration over a book contract, I knew immediately that I was similarly ungrateful. The Lord has given me great gifts, but I was focused on what He hadn't tucked into the pocket of my jeans. Instead of looking gratefully upon all that He offered, I questioned why it couldn't be just a little bit more.

I wanted $50 without even an acknowledgment of the $40 I held in my hands.

> A mountain of God is the mountain of Bashan;
> A mountain of many peaks is the mountain of Bashan.
> Why do you look with envy, O mountains with many peaks,
> At the mountain which God has desired for His abode?
> Surely the LORD will dwell there forever. (Ps. 68:15–16)

Do you see the beauty in the God-design of your life, in both the rugged and majestic places of your days? Or are you looking at the hills across the valley, wondering why God's hand of blessing is seemingly better on those green hills? This psalm of David provides a poetic balm to conflicted souls that long for more or different—in our homes and our dreams.

> When we embrace the gift of home as it really is, we fill up and spill over into the lives of our family and friends, and even out into the world.

We have each been given the children, marriages, unique abilities, financial resources, and life circumstances that God chose intentionally. For some, this may look like $40, and for others it may resemble $50. The size and scope of His gift is different for each one of us, and it's all as it should be.

When we spend the days comparing our lot in life, literally comparing our small city home with a zero lot-line to her lush acres out in the country, we miss out on the real-life delights in the gifts we've been given. However, when we embrace the gift of home as it really is, we fill up and spill over into the lives of our family and friends, and even out into the world.

> You give a gift to others by making them feel comfortable and welcomed, not by changing who you are.
>
> Melissa Michaels

Swing Wide the Doors

She'd worked her nine-to-five job all week. But early in the morning on Good Friday she planted Easter lilies along the border of her garden and hung a home-sewn banner from their front door announcing, "He is Risen, indeed!" It felt a little bold for her introverted tendencies, but all during Lent, as she quieted her heart to listen to the Lord, it was this instruction that she heard: "Let your neighbors know that you are mine."

In the days that followed, three different women stopped by unexpectedly. "I thought I was the only Christian on the block," they confided in one another. Shortly after that she decided to start a neighborhood Bible study in her home, and left a small potted plant with an invitation on every doorstep. Five women arrived the first night that they gathered. Four of them brought their Bibles. The fifth had never owned one.

Make no mistake; Christian hospitality is an art form—and you don't have to be a stay-at-home mom to dabble in this medium. The real creative block that holds us back from living hospitable lives isn't about the number of hours we live at home, but has everything to do with our contentment. It's impossible to swing wide the front door of our home lives if we are fearful that it's not good enough. Generosity cannot flow from your life until you gratefully accept what you possess, and then decide to give it away. Without contentment it is very difficult, I dare say impossible, to pour out and into the lives of neighbors and friends. How can we have them over the threshold of our front door if we keep wishing it were more . . . wishing we were more?

However, when you invite people into the private places of your home life, either online or over your dining room table, you are the living, breathing gospel to your guests. Just like Paul, confined yet unhindered. A woman at home is a full and complete picture of a redeemed life, serving others with the generosity and love that she first received. And for many creative women, hospitality is a private sort of art form without pictures being shared online, but rather simple love being given over the breaking of bread.

> Generosity cannot flow from your life until you gratefully accept what you possess, and then decide to give it away.

The gift of hospitality, when invested like the faithful servant in Christ's parable of the talents, produces a mighty harvest. It has the power to open hardened hearts, bless aching souls, heal wounded spirits, and bring rest to weary bones. And let us not forget the emphasis our Lord Himself placed on meal sharing. I love the way Brennan Manning put it:

> Sadly, the meaning of meal sharing is largely lost in the Christian community today. In the Near East, to share a meal with someone is a guarantee of peace, trust, fraternity, and forgiveness—the shared table symbolizes a shared life. An orthodox Jew's saying, "I would like to have dinner with you" is a

metaphor that implies, "I would like to enter into friendship with you." Even today an American Jew will share a doughnut and a cup of coffee with you, but to extend a dinner invitation is to say, "Come to my *mikdash me-at*, the miniature sanctuary of my dining room table where we will celebrate the most sacred and beautiful experience that life affords—friendship."

A Work in Progress

There are some women who know how to get creative on a dime and in a sliver of time. They are generous with their words and their home. Without large sums of money or ample square footage, they are taking what they have and where they live and turning it into their beauty offering. But the decorator must frame and hang this one piece of truth over the mantel of her soul: the whole home, like the whole homemaker, is a work in progress.

So she learns to let go and fall back into her mountain of throw pillows when perfectionism threatens her balance. In the midst of small shoes thrown carelessly by the back door, and the stacks of preschool art that litter and glitter her countertops, she chooses to really live. Because living—truly living—is the most beautiful art form of all.

> It doesn't have to be perfect to be beautiful.
>
> Myquillyn Smith

I believe many women with this unique gift of home stop themselves from taking on the mantle of a true artist because they've convinced themselves that they're *just homemakers*, albeit homemakers with flare. *Domestic Divas* is the fancy name they've given themselves, laughing it away as something less than. But let's blow the dust bunnies from under this lie!

Just a homemaker? I've learned that any time a person describes herself as *just* anything, she's lost sight of the simple reality that she is God's masterpiece, His fearfully and wonderfully written *poiēma* to the world. Just a homemaker, just a mom, just a crafter, just a baker, just a Pinterest junkie . . . *just* nothing!

Are you one of these creative homemakers, inspiring *me* to better love *my family* and community by *your example*? Do you know that God is using you on my darkest days, like a beacon of light? Though you may think that you're simply decorating your home and documenting your parties, you creative homemakers are inspiring me to embrace family life in living color.

And this goes for you working mothers out there too! Though you balance an office job Monday through Friday, home is still your pièce de résistance, your ultimate mission. Bravo for keeping that focus though you work beyond your home walls. Your words, your pictures and songs and recipes, and all the hard-earned advice you have to share about balance and faith build me up too. You are nothing short of amazing!

Like the singer who points us back to God's greatness, and the painter who draws our attention to the miracle of creation, homemakers actively minister to us as well. Inspired women, living inspired lives, inspiring generations from their homes. We follow them online, try new recipes, switch out throw pillows and picture frames with the seasons, and freeze miniature dinosaurs in a Tupperware of water for our children to excavate on a hot afternoon. Inspired by these ingenious creative moms living fully, quite contented, at home.

Chapter Nine

The Pull of the Tide

I will take time for a moment of pleasure and
peace, because it centers me, and I have decided
I will last longer in this very long distance race if
I build anchors of serendipity into my schedule.

Sally Clarkson

We dragged the table to the center of the porch and angled it slightly so that everyone could benefit from the view just beyond the railing. Sprawling hills surrounded a deep, blue lake that gleamed like a million diamonds in the setting sun. Feeling a nip in the Northern California air, I shivered, but it was more than the cold that brought the chill: it was the experience.

Inside, the rest of the ladies worked together to prepare that evening's meal. I heard their voices blend in a rich cacophony of joy. The occasional burst of laughter split the steady hum of conversation, and all of it combined together with the backdrop in one big glorious assault to my senses.

We had gathered for our annual creative retreat. Writers, photographers, and teachers, all six of us intent on using our artistic capabilities to bless others. For five days we pulled away from our families and took rest in California's wine country. This was where we spurred one another on to good, creative works.

Photographers left in the morning, cameras and tripods in tow, and spent their days seeking out new locations to shoot. The lake house grew quiet during daytime hours as the writers tapped away at keyboards. One gal pieced together various Shakespearean scenes for her students to perform in the coming year. Another further developed her website, providing beautiful content for her readers, while the other two worked on book ideas that had been simmering, but couldn't be developed for lack of time.

In the evenings we came together over beautifully crafted meals, and as the sun sank low behind the hills we shared our work with one another, showing pictures and reading excerpts of the work we'd accomplished that day. We provided feedback and encouragement, building one another up in the unique ways we had each been created. And when each of us laid head to pillow, we did so exhausted and refreshed from a full day of creating.

A short time of pulling away is a glorious celebration for mothers.

Dropping Anchor

There's a fear in the hearts of working women, as well as in the hearts of moms at home who dare do anything beyond mothering. We fear that our children will suffer terribly if we aren't constantly at their sides, but it's simply not true. Some of these fears stem from this helicopter age of parenting, of hovering and controlling and entertaining our child's every play, so different from how most of us grew up. Our parents didn't play with us all day. They gave us bicycles and books; we sought out friends in the neighborhood, and a pass to the city pool, and were told to come in when the streetlights came on. Today the world is different, and there's less freedom for children, which means less *apparent* freedom for moms.

But children still need space to roam, and moms need their sense of autonomy. So we get creative and help them gain independence while still close to home, in back yards and on cul-de-sacs, giving them time each day without mom's watchful eye. Setting up toy animals in a long procession down the hallway or reading good books in the crook of a tree allows little ones space to step into the freedom of their own creativity. And as the children find their footing in this world of independence, so do their mothers.

Freedom and independence are really more like *inter*dependence in a healthy family. As the ocean ebbs and flows with the pull of the tide, so do a mother's days, pulling away for a time, then gathering back close to the shore of family life. It's not always easy. In fact, it is *anything* but easy. Constantly riding the waves of change, high and low tide, looking for our rhythm. Sometimes this in-and-out pull happens gently, while other times we crash like the white-capped waves. And through it all we learn to practice our unique artistic gifts like a spiritual discipline. These are the moments when we learn to drop anchor.

> Dropping anchor into deep creative waters centers me.

Dropping anchor into deep creative waters centers me. Dropping brush into paint; dropping that calligraphy pen, bone dry for years, back into ink; dropping anchor into God's Word. Dropping down to the floor to stretch. Dropping everything to plan a date night. Dropping into deep thoughts over how He made me in His image, not only as a nurturer, but also as a creative in the midst of motherhood. Lowering the anchor, I slip into artistic waters for a sliver of time, or perhaps the better part of a school day. Maybe the children go to a friend's house to play, and I forgo the never-ending housework to edit a new batch of photos or try out a new recipe. In these moments I drop my anchor and put my hands to the other special parts of who I am: storyteller, artist, photographer; a girl who likes to make things pretty, spin a pottery wheel, curl ribbons, or simply create another digital scrapbook of memories. Then after a time, centered and filled up again, I rush back in like the faithful returning tide, refreshed and ready to serve my family again.

However, the waters can be dangerous if one doesn't understand the science of the ocean's current and dashes impulsively out into the waves. I wish I had a formula to give you, packaged pretty and ready to be applied to every artistic mother in every home, family, and unique brand of busy life, but I don't. Only a warning: marriages and children can suffer in the surf—and so we practice the pulling away and rushing in carefully, and always with the help of lifeguards.

Lifeguards

> If either of them falls, the one will lift up his companion. But woe to the one who falls when there is not another to lift him up. (Eccl. 4:10)

The term *tribe* is popular today in both parenting and creative circles because we all need a support system to do life successfully. I, however, prefer to call these people *lifeguards*. The church, with its steeple and cross, is a lifeguard tower from which God's people, devoted to the Lord and to one another, are faithfully keeping watch. Promising to help when there is need, lift when lives are weak, celebrate when there's joy, and grieve when there is loss. We function together. A body. A church.

You need lifeguards standing watch as you navigate the waters of family and art. Flesh-and-blood women to cheer you on, affirm your design, but also bold enough to call you back to shore when the tides suddenly shift and turn. Your best friend, other creatives, prayer partners, the neighbor who loves to have your kids over for playdates, your mother-in-law who flies in to help with the children when you dare produce your first art show at the coffee shop downtown. All of them lifeguards—all of them the church.

Two friends met for tea late one night. It had been well over a year since their last girls' night out because, well . . . life got busy—significantly busier for one of them as she'd taken on multiple teaching jobs and tutoring positions, along with continuing to pour into her three young children. But the thwarted friend didn't feel rejection, only concern. As they sat together they shared as only women do, traveling down rabbit holes in every direction, but never losing sight of the main themes. They hit all of them: motherhood, marriage, friendship, and the oft unspoken dreams of a woman.

When the excitement of sharing calmed, they sat back to finish their drinks and the one friend who had been watching the other from the wings over the past months asked in a gentle, prying way, "How are you managing it all?"

"Oh, you know," her friend answered with a wave of the hand, "I'm doing fine. There's a lot of juggling right now, what with the play I've been directing, the kids' afterschool activities, trying to connect with my husband in the evenings, and working . . . but I've figured out that all of these things I'm juggling are just like balls in the air. Some of the balls are rubber and some of the balls are glass, so I'm just trying to make sure I catch the glass balls, letting the rubber balls bounce when they need to." All this she said with a lopsided smile.

It was then that her old friend leaned in close, took hold of her hand, and tenderly said, "I've watched you the last few months, and I'm afraid it's possible that you've let a couple of the glass balls fall."

> Speaking the truth in love, we are to grow up in all aspects into
> Him who is the head, even Christ. (Eph. 4:15)

Speaking the truth in love is one of the most difficult parts of Christlike friendship, but it is the backbone to accountability relationships. Lifeguards are the friends who care more about our character, in all aspects of our lives, than our happiness and fulfillment. They sharpen us, as iron sharpens iron, and encourage us to keep our eyes fixed upon the Author and Perfecter of faith. Always at the ready to encourage and build us up, but also willing to do the painful work of sitting us down and speaking hard truth in gentle tones.

In Real Life

Piglet sidled up to Pooh from behind.

"Pooh!" he whispered.

"Yes, Piglet?"

"Nothing," said Piglet, taking Pooh's paw. "I just wanted to be sure of you."

A. A. Milne, *The House at Pooh Corner*

Women are social beings. We like to be sure that someone is near. Even the most introverted of our kind crave meaningful relationships. We thrive on knowing and being known, and our need to be experienced is a powerful pull—strong as the tide. It is for this reason that personal, face-to-face relationships must be cultivated and pursued. We need lifeguards IRL: in real life.

Finding these women to link arms with is trickier than it may seem. It requires that we let our guard down and reveal the messy parts of life. This can be quite hard in a photoshopped world, but we must be open to inviting others into our homes despite laundry in baskets, cluttered countertops, and a dinner table set with shredded wheat. Waiting for life to be lovelier before inviting others in can get lonely. If you want friends in real life then you must open up your real life.

If you want friends in real life then you must open up your real life.

So where do we go to find like-minded women to encourage and affirm us in these messy places of life—women who will speak the truth in love and watch over us? Where do we find lifeguards?

Friends, let's begin by turning back to the lifeguard tower: the church.

This is often where they're found—creative moms decorating the stage for the annual women's tea, teaching children's Sunday school story hour with flair, whipping up breakfast quiches for the local MOPS group, throwing baby showers, and on the list could go. Face-to-face community is where the Lord is, where He ushers in His Spirit through the prayers of a faithful gathering. In this digital age of constant communication, we sometimes forget the importance of nearness. Proximity. Hugging necks and lending hands.

> For where two or three have gathered together in My name, I am there in their midst. (Matt. 18:20)

Even if they aren't as driven as you are to begin a home-based business or redecorate every corner of the home with each changing season, you still need the experience of a real gathering, with the Lord present in your midst. But if you're still left wanting because your local community doesn't understand your drive to take your creative talents out into the world or your passion for perfecting a painting technique, then thank goodness for the option of online communities where you can find inspiring relationships to encourage you. Because while we were never intended to live our lives sitting at a computer, sometimes these online communities meet a deep need. Online we find other uniquely similar creative personalities who get us and our dreams. Yes, after telling you how crucial IRL relationships are, we're here to say that digital friendships matter too.

In Virtual Life

When Meredith Bernard quit her job to stay home with her children, she did so with the stirrings of a dream in her heart. Photography had long been an interest, but during her days at home what she had considered a hobby now began calling out to her day and night, compelling her to follow this growing passion. The path was difficult, full of second-guessing as it can often be for moms who are transitioning a hobby into a business venture.

Thoroughly overwhelmed with all that needed to be done, Meredith knew she couldn't find success without help. The ins and outs of starting a photography business were more than she could handle alone. And since she didn't have friends to call on in her small fellowship circle, she searched for community online, and found it in abundance.

"Two things were very clear to me," Meredith shared when I probed her about the support she gleaned from a small, private Facebook group for photographers. "I knew God was calling me out on this limb, and I knew it was going to be completely up to Him to keep me from falling. And He did . . . by sending me a group of women that also kept me from jumping."

For all the pitfalls we find in social media, the many blessings it provides are equally awe-inspiring. No longer isolated and alone when real-life connections cannot be found, now we have a cavernous space in which to develop community through the online sphere. Extending hands to one another through words and photos and the sharing of daily life and art, we feel safe and known. We catch a glimpse of the familiar in a like-minded woman, and with a wink and a smile we speak into the void: "I get it. I see you. Let's move forward together."

The power of digital community is buoying up artistic moms in amazing ways today. Pushing one another toward greatness in each individual pursuit, we are the lifeguards who swim out into the waves together, acknowledging that sometimes swimming out farther from shore takes courage, but we're not alone, and the water feels great.

I was eleven years old, sitting by the front door because I knew she would soon return. Dad said her flight landed at 5:00, so she should pull into the driveway any minute. Headlights cut through the dark, wintery night, and my heart leapt, because Mom was home.

I fell into her arms just as she crossed the threshold, the frigid blast of air biting at my exposed skin. Mom had been away for a retreat with a few women from our church. Young and naïve, I didn't understand why that time away was so important, but I get it now. There are so many things I remember about that night—the smell of her perfume and the way her blue eyes shined; but more than anything I remember how excited she was to see my brother and me. Mom had her tank filled in those days away, and I never forgot the joy of her return.

Your church likely offers weekend getaways each year, but there are other retreats and conferences throughout the country where friendships formed online converge in real life. This communion of fellowship happens frequently at conferences for creative artisans. In those sacred gatherings, women who have become dear to us finally draw near to us at a conference center, in a hotel lobby, on an airplane shuttle. Finally we hug each other tight and laugh together over a long-promised cup of coffee. There's something soothing about walking into a room of writers for the one whose mind constantly spins with stories. For the musician who hears melodies in her sleep, stepping into a songwriter's conference fills the deep reservoir inside her soul. For the painter, the home decorator, the baker, and all the creative souls in between, finding community in these areas of common interest lets us know we're not alone on this Renaissance path.

So dip your toes into the refreshing waters of community, my friends. Seek and find relationships IRL and digitally, and perhaps even through conferences if possible, where the two merge. It's here that you will find lifeguards waiting in the wings to cheer you on toward your creative dreams.

And always, there at the shore, are the darling little loved ones, standing guard over your family home. Yes, those miniature lifeguards who linger on the coastline may be the most important of them all.

The Littlest Lifeguards

I sat in the coffee shop and watched her walk through the door. Dressed in a flowing white maxi dress, she flipped her auburn hair and caught my eye, grinning and rushing over for a hug. Danielle Smith is beautiful on the outside and equally stunning inside. The feminine powerhouse behind Danielle Smith Media, and the voice of ExtraordinaryMommy.com, an online site dedicated to cultivating and curating positive stories from around the web. We sat across from each other, I with my hot tea, and she with her latte, and we dove in, excited to catch up after not seeing one another for some time. It was only natural that two writers would eventually fall onto the topic of our work.

Danielle is not just a writer, but she's also gifted in front of the camera. Before vlogging was a thing, Danielle offered her wisdom in short, well-edited video clips. Companies took notice, and now Danielle flies all over the world as a brand representative, sharing her unique talent of reporting and speaking through her videos. But success comes with a price, especially when you're a mother.

"It's a competitive field," Danielle told me when I asked her what it was like to represent so many different brands. "I'm not the only one doing this anymore, and I have two young kids, which means I have to find a way to work in a field that I love while also maintaining order at home. And now that the kids are older, I've found that it's important, both to them and to me, to include them in some of my business decisions."

She paused for a moment, gazing out the window so that the morning sunlight reflected in her eyes. Turning back, she offered me a small smile. "Bringing the kids into the business has kept me centered, and it's given them a sense of ownership in what I do."

Weeks before our meeting, Danielle received a call with a wonderful opportunity. The work would require that she leave home for a few days, and as she looked at the calendar she realized that this particular project would have her away on her son's birthday. She wrestled with the decision for several days before finally going to her boy and asking his opinion.

"He was so attentive as I gave him the details of the job," she told me. Her finger traced the side of her mug slowly as the memory of that conversation played out in her mind. "I just asked him how he would feel if I wasn't there for his birthday, and I made it clear that he could give me his honest answer, because I wanted him to know that his opinion mattered."

With a giant, lopsided grin, Danielle's little boy looked up at his mom from beneath his mop of blond hair and gave her his blessing to take the job. "That sounds really cool, Mom!" he exclaimed. "We can celebrate my birthday when you get home."

Danielle left a few days later without a hint of guilt, having been given the freedom to enjoy her work by her littlest lifeguard. And because God cares about our sacrifices, the small and the large ones, it happened that her project wrapped earlier than expected, and Danielle made it home on her son's birthday just before he went to bed.

Children act as lifeguards without even trying. Sometimes their contented joy reminds you that all is safe and well. But when family gets thrown off-kilter, they'll be the first to sound an alarm. If and when focus is pulled too far from that familial shore, you can rest assured the kids will let you know it. Be ever watchful for signs that maybe they need more of you—behavioral issues, emotions run askew, or simple neediness. It could be as simple as offering extra minutes of snuggles and conversation at bedtime instead of rushing to the computer, or sitting on the back patio eating a popsicle in the mid afternoon rather than answering that call.

Or maybe, like Danielle, you need to bring your kids further into your creative business and ministry dreams, allowing them to sleeve prints and ship orders, sell books at conferences, or take pictures for your Etsy site. Invite them into the waters with you, so that those dreams you have aren't threatening to them, like a dangerous riptide pulling you out of their reach, out of their sight.

But still, even still . . . even when you've been wise and all seems to be working well, a mom can know overwhelming guilt.

The Deep Waters of Guilt

> But the Helper, the Holy Spirit, whom the Father will send in My name, He will teach you all things, and bring to your remembrance all that I said to you. (John 14:26)

I got hungry for their faces one afternoon as I ran around the neighborhood. It came upon me suddenly like the crashing of a wave, and I quickly made my way back home only to find them crisscross-applesauce around Legos, singing "Jungle Boogie" with their dad.

Working out is healthy for my body and my mind. As crazy as it sounds, though, the hardest part of making this healthy commitment is not a lack of self-motivation to get out, but the self-guilt holding me in.

Still, I'm learning that pulling away and doing something healthy for my body is good and right and balancing, again like dropping anchor. That's why pulling away for a time is a spiritual discipline, because when we return, we do so refreshed and ready, healthy and whole.

If our early mothering years are the Dark Ages before the Renaissance, then guilt is the Great Plague that takes us down altogether. And nothing causes guilt for a mother of young children faster than this idea of pulling away—dropping anchor at a conference full of like-minded women, pulling away for a morning run before the family gets rolling, diving into an online class, navigating your way into a new work schedule, or starting back to school to get your master's degree in creative writing. As mothers, we second-guess the money, worry about the time, and feel conflicted each time we desire to do anything away from the children during these precious mothering days. It can be utterly exhausting.

> If our early mothering years are the Dark Ages before the Renaissance, then guilt is the Great Plague.

Guilt has the power to destroy your dream life and your home life and your love life. Dreams are like fuel, propelling us forward into every living corner of our days. Guilt weighs us down and, if not kept in check, stealthily robs us of our joy, stifles creativity, and succumbs to bitterness. Guilt is *not* one of our lifeguards.

Read this carefully: God does not speak in guilt. He doesn't communicate with such confusing syllables. The Lord's lips drip with freedom and forgiveness, even in the times we fail. It's in those moments when we misinterpret or misunderstand His plans for us that we come face-to-face with His life-giving grace. Gentle and kind is the way He gathers us back to shore; like a mother saving her children from the dashing of the waves. But a tender mother would never pull her child from the cruel waters only to leave them shivering in the whipping wind. Guilt is that great wind, cold and heavy on our souls.

Conviction. Conviction is the dialect He chooses. Light and direct, purposeful as the fine point of a scalpel, pointing out with precision where we've gone astray. It's important to note, however, that the line between guilt and conviction is paper thin, and can easily be blurred if we're not intimately seeking Him. I know I've encouraged you to seek Him in other places in this book, but the theme must return over and over again like the tide we speak of, so that the rip current doesn't pull us under.

We must quiet our hearts and listen carefully to see if the Lord is speaking to us with clear, convicting tones. And as we do so, we must constantly use the discernment offered freely through the Holy Spirit, communicating ceaselessly with Him, to understand each situation for what it is—an opportunity to wade out into the still waters of His grace in any and all sanctified moments of life.

It's here that I leave you with the truth of the Holy Spirit, who is the safest and surest Lifeguard of all. This is where you can test the raging waters of life that threaten to pull you under.

Chapter Ten

When God Calls a Mother

> There are things *only you* can do, and you are
> alive to do them. In the great orchestra we call
> life, you have an instrument and a song, and
> you owe it to God to play them both sublimely.
>
> Max Lucado

As her sons grew up surfing the white-capped waters of Oahu's North Shore, Monica Swanson wrote about their island life, cleverly dubbing herself "The Grommom." *Grom* is a term of endearment used to describe a young surfer, and beach moms around the world followed her online adventures as she mothered her four boys. Between surf competitions and homeschool days, Monica wrote about parenting and life on their little island property, about the fruit they harvested and the organic meals she prepared. In those early days of blogging, all she knew was that she'd found passion and purpose at the keyboard, sharing bits of their life with the small community that chose to read along.

One day, as Monica sat at the computer editing photos to share, her husband passed by and stopped, leaning down to observe her work. Her fingers slowed as he watched, and in the brief silence, he casually asked, "So, a hobby or a job?" Defenses immediately went up as she tried to decipher what he meant. Did she need to justify any moment she took for herself? Was he expecting her to make money if she was spending time doing anything else other than mothering? Her husband didn't ask his question with aggression, but still she felt attacked. She spouted some words back that she instantly regretted, and the conversation was over.

Over the next few days, Monica worked to formulate her plans for her blog into a clear couple of sentences that her husband would understand. With a date night planned, she bided her time rather than broaching the topic again. When the night arrived they drove down the coast to their favorite restaurant on the water. Sitting together, watching the sun sink low, she dared give voice to her dreams.

"You asked me about my blog the other day and I've been thinking about it," she began. "Right now all I know is that I really enjoy writing to women and encouraging them in their marriages and in parenting. I love using the pictures that you and the boys take of the beach and the house. Putting these posts together inspires me to be a better wife, totally engaged with the kids, and to try new things in the kitchen and with decorating. Also, in a house full of men it's really fulfilling to have these online relationships with women. I don't know if I'll ever make money off of this. Maybe. But right now, I really just enjoy what I'm doing."

"Oh," her husband said with a nod. "That makes sense. I want to support you any way I can. So how can I help?" The very next post Monica wrote went viral. That was about the time I met her.

Monica and the kids were on the mainland for a national surf competition, cheering on her third-born son, the child with the sandy hair and sun-kissed skin. Because I lived nearby, I brought my own children down to the beach to join the excitement. As Monica and I sat together on a towel later that afternoon, I asked her about the recent explosion of followers on her site. Where once she had a small, loyal following of other beach moms, now it seemed to be overflowing with traffic from women all over the world. I wanted to know what she'd done differently—what big changes she'd made, what big prayers she had prayed. She simply answered my question by sharing the story of that date night with her husband.

"I was finally able to communicate with my husband what I was doing and why I wanted to keep doing it, and he told me that he understood and supported me fully, and then BAM!"

"It's almost like he gave you his blessing," I said in the space that followed.

Monica nodded back in agreement. "I've actually said those exact words before. Once I had Dave's blessing, everything began to fall into place."

As I watched them load up their things at the end of our beach day, I thought of the sacrifice they all made to pursue her third-born son's dreams. Surfing competitions take them to new locations, traveling from hotels, to the beach, and back again day after day. But they're committed to doing this together. Her son's unique talent drives them all to attack his dream as if it were their own.

That's often what we do with our children when they have a specific gift; we get together with our loved ones and attempt to figure out the road that will lead them to where they want to go. And we do the same thing late at night with our husbands when they're contemplating a career change or a long-suppressed passion that's quaking beneath the surface and

> Listening to and rooting our loved ones on is second nature for many of us.

threatening to undo them if they don't give it a try—like quitting a secure job to go back to school for a master's degree in counseling, or finding investors for a new company. Listening to and rooting our loved ones on is second nature for many of us.

But what happens when God calls a mother? When the dreams of our creative hearts begin bubbling to the surface, suddenly the whole affair seems private and risky as feelings of guilt push to the surface, because shouldn't we be satisfied just raising these precious souls? So we often shove the dreams down deep, or we write them off as hobbies, and refuse to communicate what we really desire outside of motherhood. Or maybe we communicate these desires poorly, at the wrong time, blowing up defensively late at night. Other times we try our best to share our hearts, but those who love us don't know what they can do to help—and the conversation ends before it truly begins.

That's about the time Mom starts sneaking it in, the writing and the singing and the painting, dipping slowly into her creativity in the slivers of stolen time. Eventually, there's a song she's composed or an online shop she's opened or a children's book she's written and illustrated all by herself on the computer. It's fun and she's proud of herself, and the kids and her husband are surprised and proud of her too, and life continues on without change. That is until Mom's creative outlet starts costing the family more time and a little bit of money. That's when husbands are usually ready to communicate.

I don't write that with a condescending tone, because I don't blame our men for not understanding what we've dreamed up during all those middle-of-the-night feedings. Time and again, this is how I've seen the dreams of a mom make their way up and out of the dark ages and into the light of the Renaissance.

Slowly.

Timidly.

Sometimes defensively.

But we can't be afraid of the questions, because more often than not they come from the people who love us most. We interpret the questions as pressure, but it's not pressure if we learn to properly interpret our family's curiosities.

Usually the people closest to us simply want to understand what's going on, what we're thinking and hoping to do, and how we plan to manage everything else that begs for our time each day. So the questions come from our moms who didn't experience motherhood in a digital age the way that we are, where work was clearly separated from the home and you either did one or the other, but rarely both.

Maybe the questions come from the kids who want to know why

we get to spend long chunks of time on the computer when they're only allowed thirty minutes of screen time each day. They don't value the creative nature of the art simply because they don't understand it. Consider this your opportunity to bring them into your dreams and figure it out together.

Most likely your husband's inquisitions aren't accusatory either, but rather a simple desire to understand what excites you. If you don't bring him into the beauty of your artistic offering, and share with him why it's so important to you, then he's left to make his own judgment from the periphery, and for nonartistic husbands this can all seem odd and confusing.

Called Together

> But at the beginning of creation God "made them male and female." "For this reason a man will leave his father and mother and be united to his wife, and the two will become one flesh." So they are no longer two, but one flesh. Therefore what God has joined together, let no one separate. (Mark 10:6–9 NIV)

Christmas Eve, and the night was clear. Our church asked if I'd deliver a dramatic monologue based on the gospel accounts of Jesus's birth at all four of their evening services. Talking this through with my husband, we decided that I'd say yes. I had traveled up and down the coast to other churches that year, but hadn't yet served in our local community.

As the beautiful cacophony of strings and woodwinds warmed up in the background before the first service, our pastor sat down in the pew next to me and said with his deep, resonating tones, "I want you to thank your husband for sharing you with us tonight."

I hemmed and hawed and downplayed his words by saying, "Oh, my mom's there. I bet they won't miss me at all." But his hand went to my arm, and he smiled.

"When our children were young," he said, "I felt God call me to the foreign mission field. I learned very quickly that when God calls one person to ministry, He calls a whole family. I want you to thank your husband for us when you get home."

Dear friends, I encourage you to include your husband, your children, and the loved ones who support you in this inspired life you're living. Don't think of your budding dreams as something you've been called to do alone. Share your scribbled-down dreams with them. Go to them for counsel, let them help you set healthy boundaries, and learn together how to answer the call God has on your life. For when God calls a mother, He calls a whole family.

> When God calls a mother, He calls a whole family.

When I scroll through my Instagram feed, I always stop to gaze at her photos. They're bright, engaging, and joy-filled. They show a simple vase of flowers against a white backdrop, the cute shoes she wore to drop her son at school, or the loving gaze of a mother looking into her son's eyes.

Lisa Leonard is a jewelry designer, a photographer, a mother and wife, and the powerhouse behind Lisa Leonard Designs where she offers beautiful, hand-stamped jewelry, perfect for every occasion. Like many small businesses, Lisa Leonard Designs began with one woman lovingly crafting and selling each piece on her own. Today, however, Lisa works with a team—people in her home, in her local community, and even on the opposite side of the globe.

Lisa is a beautiful example of what can happen when this digital Renaissance propels us into our Great Commission call. Taking her gifts beyond her own personal realm, she is sharing the gospel-infused message of compassion and care by hiring and training Dominican women and men to make jewelry, providing them with a safe work environment, a marketable skill, and a sustainable income; and all this stems from one creative woman's gift shared with the world.

This is the hands-and-feet offering of an artistic mother, when art turns more than a simple financial profit, but also the profit of touching and changing lives. Lisa knows, however, that she could never have orchestrated this on her own. Because you see, before God called Lisa to the task of making and selling jewelry, He called her to her husband.

Lisa is the first to admit that there would be no Lisa Leonard Designs without Steve Leonard. When she began turning her hobby of making jewelry into a business, Steve didn't just give her his blessing, he also blessed her with his business know-how. He's the glue, the brains behind her creative genius. This is because early on *she invited him in.* Each time Steve noticed and admired his wife's work, she asked his advice on the business dealings. Through conflict, triumph, and change, Lisa and Steve have partnered together to build something meaningful.

Today, Steve Leonard serves as the company's CEO. He manages their team and financials as well as oversees marketing, website construction and function, and vision casting for future projects. This frees Lisa up to do what she does best—create jewelry and nurture her family.

It's important that we recognize our own limitations, as well as the strengths of others in our family. Partnering with our husbands, knowledgeable friends or family members, and any other support system who can fill in the gaps where we're lacking frees us up to dive fully into the skill that got us started in the first place. A creative woman's talent, paired with the wisdom and guidance of her support network, has the power to propel her out into the world.

This isn't to say that your husband will immediately jump into the pilot seat of your creative endeavor, *or that he'll jump in at all.* Some won't ever catch the vision for what we want to do, or they might not have the know-how that we lack, or they're just too busy with their own careers.

It's easy to get hurt feelings when you feel a passion for something that your husband doesn't share, but chances are the man you married wasn't bent on destroying your dreams or squashing your success, and that isn't his goal

> Creative woman, your husband is for you, not against you . . . even if he doesn't always understand you.

now. Creative woman, your husband is for you, not against you . . . even if he doesn't always understand you. You are two different personalities there in one flesh, and it can rub something awful. Still, if you feel called by God to something more, then you've been called to do more *together*.

She said the words and I gasped audibly, because her words acknowledged an inner struggle that I'd never before voiced.

"He was so excited for me, and for the opportunities opening up before me, and he communicated his excitement with more enthusiasm than I'd ever heard from him before. And I panicked."

Angie Smith is a writer, a speaker, and the mother of four energetic girls. She is also married to Todd Smith, the lead singer of the Grammy Award–winning group Selah. These are people who understand the melding of creativity, faith, and family, and the tightrope we walk between opportunity and overcommitment.

Angie's words came through the telephone as a cacophony of sound played behind both of us. I was trapped inside a hotel room with my baby (whom I caught splashing in the toilet as I spoke on the phone) while she sat tucked away in the quietest corner of her home, her daughters and their friends shrieking with delighted laughter in the background. There we were, a picture of this book—two creative women whispering words of encouragement to one another's creative souls, as the sound track of motherhood played loud around us.

"My husband is so proud of me, and I find a lot of comfort in that. But there was a time early on when opportunities started pouring in faster and faster that I misconstrued his excitement to be obligation. And suddenly I felt this immense, suffocating pressure to keep building momentum. But that was never his intention. He was *just* excited."

I nodded so hard my neck began to hurt, because I have experienced the same feelings. My husband is my number one cheerleader, and he's quick to offer help and encouragement for every opportunity that comes my way. But at times I've wondered if I let him down by not doing more. His excitement became my fear, and that was never his intention.

Angie went on, "As I began to feel more and more anxiety over the many opportunities coming at me, Todd took notice and got me away for a few days to talk through it all. It became clear to both of us that an open dialogue was key to maintaining my sanity, as well as our connection."

She continued as I picked up the baby and bounced her on my hip, wiping the toilet water off her chubby hands, and hoping to keep her quiet a little longer as I gleaned nuggets of wisdom from this woman I so admired.

"What I've learned these last few years is that there will always be opportunity out there, and a lot of it is in areas that I'm perfectly qualified to fill. But there are a lot of other women who are also totally capable of filling those spots, writing those words, and speaking at those events." I put the baby back down, dropping a few Cheerios on the floor in front of her so I could furiously scribble Angie's words on a notepad.

"And then there are opportunities that the Lord has placed before me, that only *I* can fill," she continued, her voice gentle. "Being wife to Todd; being mom to my girls. No one else can fill those spots. And so I have given myself the freedom to say no to opportunities that can easily be filled by someone else. Saying no has allowed me to say yes to the opportunities right here in front of me."

After this call, as I washed my child off in the hotel room bathtub, I considered the wide range of marriages represented in this Renaissance. Some of them have ended, others of them are persevering but strained, some are strong and thriving, others are just surviving. But all of them need communication.

Even with communication, some of you may experience hardship within your marriages. Perhaps you feel unseen or your desires go unmet. I recognize this challenge and offer this encouragement: live on your knees.

As I mentioned previously, God never meant for your creativity to be sacrificed on the altar of motherhood, nor does He desire to see it sacrificed on the altar of marriage. But He does long to see His children live in obedience. If your husband is unsupportive of your creative offering, then set it aside for a time and pray faithfully for the Lord to make His timing known. If God wants to use your gift to His glory, He will make it possible to do so without dishonoring your husband. In the meantime, pray faithfully and use your creative gift right there in your Jerusalem to bless not only your children but also your husband. This is as blessed an offering as any you could give.

It Starts at Home with Him

He went to bed without me, tired from his workday while mine was just beginning. Now that the house was finally still, I had writing on my mind. There was a post to finish, a book to outline, and a talk to prepare for. With the children in bed for the night I could finally put ink to paper. But one step closer to those goals can mean a step back from my beloved. And sometimes that step feels more like a great divide.

My husband is the constant by my side, forever affirming my gifts and talents both as a mother and as a creative woman. He is the one I turn to when I'm unsure if I'm on the right path, the one who makes me feel alive with purpose in my day-to-day endeavors. But he is also the easiest one for me to place on the back burner of importance. He's self-sufficient—not like the children who need my constant care. How quickly I can forget that he needs me as much as I need him.

And so in this Renaissance rebirth, as I begin to live again, I must remind myself to keep my husband a priority too, because he can get lost just as quickly as I can. And marriages get lost too. Isn't that frightening? And haven't we already experienced it to some degree? So I write these words to myself as I write them to you, fellow Renaissance moms. As new dreams begin to clamor at the shores of our souls, and creative outlets begin calling, let's be careful not to go all Thelma and Louise on this inspired life, leaving our men in the dust as we peel away from the curb. We cannot let the artistic gospel work being done beyond our walls strangle the gospel picture God created marriage to reflect.

This is both a literal and figurative charge. We can peel away from him physically, sitting down to the computer or sewing machine, night after night. Or we can leave him emotionally, because our love for self-expression has taken over as soul mate.

There are myriad ways we can forsake our spouses in a quest to get to a music rehearsal, a speaking engagement, a bake sale, a writer's group, another photography session, or a flea market to find new pieces to refinish.

> We cannot let the artistic gospel work being done beyond our walls strangle the gospel picture God created marriage to reflect.

Dear friends, let me say it this way: what a price we pay when our passions become our priority. Your love for do-it-yourself projects doesn't mean you were intended to do it all alone. Purpose and plan to make your husband your priority again, and you may both discover what good works God has planned for you together.

I met Jenni and her husband, Kevin, shortly after our family moved to town, and I was immediately drawn to her humor, her sweet nature, and her darling kids. Not long after our families became acquainted, my husband and I began meeting regularly with Jenni and Kevin for a weekly Bible study, both of our families working through unique challenges and new callings in our marriages. It was during this time of meeting that I first discovered Jenni's love for photography. She shared her deep passion for capturing God's creation through the lens of her camera that Friday night with tears shining in her eyes.

"I don't know what to do with this," she said with a shaking voice. A homeschool mother of three young kids, Jenni didn't see a future in her craft, but she felt a constant pull to further study and pursue it. The two halves of herself seemed to contradict one another.

Likewise, Kevin contemplated a huge career change—something that would completely alter the way they had lived and operated as a family: leaving the corporate world and heading into full-time mission work. They were conflicted at every turn, wrestling through these questions until they did something radical: they sold their home and most of their belongings, bought a camper, and embarked on a yearlong tour of the United States with kids and camera in tow.

It was in this year of pulled-back surrender that Jenni's creative gift, and Kevin's pull toward ministry, began to form a very unique partnership. In the free spaces, where time and surroundings provided ample room for thoughts, Kevin knew the time to fully transition from his work as a mechanical engineer was now, while Jenni felt certain her faithfulness of studying and practicing photography were walking into fertile years of fruition.

Upon returning from this adventure, Kevin and Jenni packed a U-Haul and moved permanently to Colorado to begin working with Engineering Ministries International—Kevin using his skills as an engineer to help develop impoverished areas worldwide, and Jenni using photography to bring EMI's unique work to life.

When God calls a woman, He calls a whole family. Jenni knew her talent for photography was not to be wasted, but there were long desert years when she didn't know what to do with this love for her art. It was in those years that she was simply faithful to the talent. She studied photography, and learned new skills in editing and videography. She was quietly watchful in the waiting, and in turn the Lord was faithful to reveal His desire for His daughter in the perfect time. And side by side with her husband and children, Jenni now offers her creative gift back to the world.

It Starts at Home with Them

"Hey, Mom? When your book comes out, can I help with your book signings? Like, can I be there at the table and hand out books and stuff?"

I glanced over at him sitting in the passenger seat beside me, his sandy blond hair gelled just so, because he's coming to an age when appearance matters and people might be looking. But it's hard for me not to see the chubby cheeked little boy who gregariously lisped his way through each day until I begged him to stop talking for just a few minutes because "Mommy's ears are hurting."

"Of course you can!" I exclaimed, and he smiled, excited to know he would have a part in the launch of this book. And why wouldn't he? He's been here every step of the way. Many of his mornings were spent snuggled up in the chair next to mine as I tapped out stories and blog posts. He was the one who asked questions when I sat back in frustration because the words wouldn't flow the way I wanted. He was there then, and he will be there when it culminates in printed pages.

> The art that you create, and the time you spend creating, isn't yours alone, but rather a shared endeavor.

The art that you create, and the time you spend creating, isn't yours alone, but rather a shared endeavor. While it's crucial to include our husbands in this creative journey, it is also important for us to bring our children into the adventure—to let them see our toil and labor, taste the fruit, and learn alongside us as we set healthy boundaries. Let them witness the way we power down, stepping off-line again, that we might focus intentionally on them and our home.

Bringing children into life's celebrations over success as well as disappointments over rejection is good, as it's all part of life together as a team. No man is an island, and neither is a creative mother. While you were no doubt uniquely designed for individual good works, you are also a one-of-a-kind puzzle piece, completing your precious family. Without you there would be a big gaping hole.

Life and art and ministry must all be a family affair.

Chapter Eleven

A Business of Art in the Busyness of Motherhood

I remember hearing God say, "Joanna, there's going to come a time where I'm going to say for you to go, and I'm going to need you to step out and go."

Joanna Gaines

eaning her head back against the wall, she let the tears fall. Coursing down flushed cheeks, a river of exhaustion flowed, dripping hot from her chin, dotting her shirt with what she believed was her own salty failure.

Tucked away in their tiny RV bathroom, the breast pump whirred, drawing from her the nourishment her daughter needed, but really it felt as though her very life was being tugged from her body. Singer-songwriter Ellie Holcomb had hit the proverbial wall, overcome with exhaustion as she lived out the desires of her heart, *all* the desires of her heart, all in one short season. Traveling with her husband, writing music, and performing felt like a dream come true, but the dream of motherhood was happening at the exact same time, and the glory crash of too many blessings left Ellie spent and fragile.

Hitting the road shortly after Emmylou was born felt right, and it *was*. But right doesn't always mean easy, and on this day Ellie was overwhelmed by it all, worn down, exhausted from the day in, day out travel with a baby as the wheels on the bus went round and round.

"Lord," the words fell from her lips in a trembled whisper. "Lord, I'm tired. I'm so tired. What do I do? Please, Lord. Please talk to me."

The silence that followed was only slightly lessened by the rhythmic hum of the pump, drawing out, taking more of her. And in the fatigue of the moment, the whisper came. So soft: *Go lie down. Take a nap.*

Shaking her head with a sigh, she unplugged the pump and screwed the lid tightly on the bottle. She looked in the mirror, circles under dewy eyes, and wondered if she'd really heard Him, or if it was simply exhaustion pulling her to the warmth of the waiting bunk.

Walking slowly past her sleeping infant, tucked snug in the car seat, Ellie slipped the bottle into the miniature fridge then laid her head down on the pillow and slept. The nap was only a picture of what God was really asking her to do. When she woke up, refreshed and more clear-minded, she lay still for a long time, looking up at the ceiling and considering all that lay ahead. A full year of touring with a baby felt like a daunting task, and so once more she whispered her prayer: "Lord, what do I do?"

In the stillness of the moment, she felt Him speak, the whisper soft like a breeze. *You are my daughter, and I have given you good gifts. You've had your rest. It's time to share the gifts now. Keep going. And don't you worry, I'm going to take* such *good care of you.*

"But what about Emmylou, Lord? I'm still learning how to be a mom. How do I travel, and tour, and work, and be a mom at the same time?"

And the wind blew. *Emmylou is your daughter, but she's my daughter first. So don't worry. I'm going to take such good care of her too.*

With a new confidence, Ellie released her fears and embraced the task before her—touring North America with her husband. For the next twelve months, Drew and Ellie Holcomb made frequent stops performing in thirty-two states and Canada, all with their growing daughter by their side. And at night as the wheels on the bus continued to spin, Ellie scratched out melodies and lyrics as inspiration clamored at her heart.

As that first year of touring came to a close, God made it clear that the time had come for Ellie to return home to Nashville. No longer content to be strapped into her car seat for long stretches of time, Emmylou needed the freedom to stretch her toddler wings, and Ellie felt the stirrings of a new call pricking at the surface of her heart. So with a kiss and a wave, she and Emmylou returned home while Drew continued to tour, and mother and daughter found solace in the predictability of routine.

Ellie drifted back to the weathered notebook of lyrics and melody lines, reading daily through the words that she had penned during those long months on the tour bus. These poetic love songs were unique, and when she'd written them she had assumed that they would remain private, a legacy gift for her little family, not one to share with the world.

The Lord, of course, had a different plan. He issued forth an unexpected invitation through the heartfelt encouragement of her husband: *Refresh the hearts of my people through these songs.* Though they had been penned for her own child, God intended them for a wider audience, *His* children. Still she worried and wondered: Why would He call her home only to call her right back out again? Recording these songs meant long days in the studio, which required that she leave her daughter home with a nanny, and the fear of the unknown began to press on her heart. Then she remembered the words the Lord had spoken to her on the tour bus months earlier: *You are my daughter, and I have given you good gifts. You've had your rest. It's time to share the gifts now. And don't you worry, I'm going to take* such *good care of you.*

Stepping off that tour bus with a baby on her hip and going home had been Ellie's first surrendered yes. When she gave in and again said yes to God's unconventional plans for her family, she returned with her daughter walking by her side, and together they watched as her first solo album jumped to the top of the charts. The refreshing words and lyrics that had filled her soul during the long months of touring became the album that would launch her career as a solo artist.

The faithful offerings of a creative mother *willing to say yes.*

> Then Jesus said to His disciples, "If anyone wishes to come after Me, he must deny himself, and take up his cross and follow Me." (Matt. 16:24)

We've spoken at length on the miracle and celebration of motherhood. We know that our children, our most beautiful creations, are our first ministry. We know that our *yes* to motherhood comes with sacrifice and a laying-down of our own desires for a time. We understand the importance of being sanctified in God's Word, and living sanctified lives, and we are fully committed to adorning the gospel with both our creativity and our godly character. But today, oh friends—today we're going to step forward into our particular gifting and talk about being creative businesswomen. It's time to shed the fear and walk forward with confidence, recognizing that there's no greater time for artistic moms to take on the title of entrepreneur, or *Mompreneur* as some have called it.

When the Lord opens the door and says, "Now is the time," we can be sure that our walking forward is under the banner of His blessing.

This chapter is your take-a-deep-breath, hold-your-chin-up, here-we-go call to freedom. Though it can be confusing to wait upon the Lord, listening for when and where and how much, I want you to be ready to answer with a surrendered yes when He does lead you out. If He calls you to develop a creative business in the midst of motherhood, I pray that you're able to clearly hear His voice and see His invitation as a blessing rather than a burden. Because when the Lord opens the door and says, "Now is the time," we can be sure that our walking forward is under the banner of His blessing. And so we prepare ourselves to say, "Yes, Lord."

Yes, I'll slow down and take a nap.

Yes, I'll go home and focus on the children.

Yes, I'll pick up my pen and write.

Yes, I'll begin selling this handspun yarn.

Yes, I'll start a business.

Yes, Lord, I believe that all of this is my Renaissance worship.

Laying down what we had planned, we choose to go where He leads. To offer up what we thought these mothering years would look like, giving our children fully to Him and accepting that they are His, and so are we.

And He is going to take *such* good care of us.

Creative Artists Versus Creative Thinkers

The children whooped and hollered like wild animals, taking turns on the zip line and then pushing one another into the pool. Noodles were used as weapons and half-consumed glasses of lemonade and remnants of lunch littered the patio table. Too much boy energy for me! I stood up, smiled at my husband who didn't seem to mind the volume or the mess, and left the yard to walk the long driveway to our mailbox. The day was warm and the earth smelled sweet.

When I pulled the hatch down and peered inside, my heart took a leap. Cardboard boxes in the mailbox can do that to a girl who likes presents—even when it's a present she bought herself using Amazon Prime's two-day shipping. But this present wasn't one I'd purchased for myself. It was a true gift, sent from a new friend.

Inside my air-conditioned kitchen with lime green countertops, I slit the box open with kitchen shears and pulled out two delicate jars, swaddled in bubble wrap. "Very Berry Preserves. Raspberry Caramel Jam." I mouthed the names, then set them down gingerly. As providence would have it, my pantry and fridge were stocked up with everything I needed to make fresh scones. So I did.

Vicki Miller had been following my blog for some time, and wanted to send me a thank-you gift for having encouraged her. She'd left her sweet offer to ship me her homemade preserves on an Instagram thread.

Surprised, touched, and curious, I sent her a private message with my home address.

Nothing kindles a friendship better than breaking bread together, except maybe slathering that bread in cream and jam! Though we weren't truly together, good cellular reception allowed us to have our tea party anyway. Yes, I called her later that afternoon as I sat down to tea and scones, her opened jars of sweet preserves laid out in front of me, and I thanked her for her generous gift. After a few minutes of talking, I pressed deeper into the conversation, because I wanted to know more about this soft-spoken woman with the deliciously generous heart.

"Have you always been creative?" I asked, and she laughed awkwardly, like I'd asked her to dance and she didn't know how. "Creative? I can't even draw a stick figure," was all she could muster on the other side of her embarrassment.

I looked again at the elegant label wrapped around the jar in front of me, then licked my spoon clean. "Okay, so you're not creative," I said, choosing to let her comment about stick people be the litmus test for what defined creativity. "Well then, why don't you tell me how you started making these preserves?" I screwed the top back on the jar and waited for the story, because there had to be one behind this scrumptious jam and the farmer's wife who had just denied that her culinary giftedness was anything artistic.

"My husband's grandma was named Mary Cherry, like the fruit," Vicki began. "Her maiden name, however, was Mary Weary. So when she married, she went from Weary to Cherry." I laughed out loud, and told her that I was digging into the Raspberry Caramel Jam for the first time. "Be careful," she teased, "there's caramel moonshine there." More laughter, more jam.

"So I married her grandson, a farmer, and realized I had some things to learn, and preserving was one of those things. So I asked Grandma Mary Cherry to teach me to freeze summer peaches and corn. Not long after, I asked a friend to show me how to make preserves. After a crash course, I was hooked. So you see, I'm not exceptionally creative. I just wanted to learn to do a few things in a farm kitchen."

Is there anything more delightful than a good story served up with a sweet treat? So I let this supposedly noncreative woman go on with her tale. "Around the time I came up with my blackberry sage preserves something clicked, you know? Suddenly I just wanted to try all sorts of flavors and combinations." I smiled as I listened to her talk it all out, because my new friend didn't know that the thing that clicked deep inside of her was creativity! Let's call her a late bloomer, but bloom she did, and all of it happening after she became a mother.

Many of us have known we were artistic from a very early age. Growing up we were ice dancers and ballerinas, we hosted tea parties with imaginary friends and sang in the church choir, we choreographed dances and wrote our own plays, then invited neighborhood children to our opening-afternoon performances. It was natural how childhood creativity flowed in our youth. However, there are others who've never felt a single surge of artistic inspiration before having children of their own. "I'm not a creative," these women often say with a shrug, and I understand the fight to reconcile this notion of creativity with the more hardwired nature built into some of you reading this book.

But remember what we stated earlier: all of us were made in the creative image of Christ. Whether you grew up twirling in your tutu, embracing your creative in-His-image design early on, or spent years organizing your books and making to-do lists, you were still created creative. Of course, some creative women are obvious artists, splashing colors and shaking tambourines, while others are creative thinkers, creative problem solvers, with creative minds that perceive the world's deep needs and imagine products and services to meet those longings. In fact, it is these nontraditional creators like my friend Vicki who are using their newfound passions to turn the stay-at-home-mom status on its ear. They're pairing their artistic gifting with their logical marketing know-how, and launching homespun creative businesses. And with the benefit of social media backing them up, they're showing the world the business-savvy power of an entrepreneurial mom.

There is a chasm-like difference between creative artists and creative thinkers. It's important to recognize these differences and accept where you may fall on the spectrum. Many lifelong creative artists have a miserable time getting things done. I know this because I am one of them. Constantly inspired but easily distracted, I find it difficult to ever get to the end of a single project. Just as I'm ramping up one newly inspired idea, another washes over me, begging for my attention, and I'll follow the wind of inspiration, forever chasing, but never quite catching.

Creative thinking entrepreneurs, however, know how to catch the inspiration, and then direct it in orderly steps. They came home from their careers to mother, and in the midst of their home-dwelling days tapped into a creative power they didn't know they possessed. Creative minds inspired and reeling from all the potential to create opportunities right where they are. Leading the charge, they're showing the rest of us how to start home businesses out of our pantries, our linen closets, and from behind computer screens.

But before we get too practical about how to follow the entrepreneurial lead here in this golden age of creativity, let's remember that there's no one way for every creative mom to launch a home business in the busyness of motherhood. Like Ellie Holcomb, drawn to the end of her physical strength, we must all cry out to the Lord, "What do You want from me?"

And then we must be prepared to say *yes*.

The Surrendered Yes

I think of my friend Vicki and her jams and her Midwestern farmer and the specific choice they made to have her stay home to raise their children. Vicki wasn't looking for a business. In fact, she still isn't certain that she even wants one. But the bubbling fruit and sugar on the stove has been a slow simmer sort of start for her little company, *MessMakerBaker*. Organic as the fruit she uses, her home canning business has grown. But when I asked about her "business," Vicki fell silent, so I pried a little deeper. Turns out, Vicki is in a love-hate relationship with the idea of calling this thing she does a business. "I had this plan of being at home," she said, "fully engaged with the kids. And now, what happens to that?"

How I wanted to reach through the phone and take hold of my new friend's hands, but instead I cradled it closer as I looked out the window to the back yard where my kids were still running and playing themselves into an afternoon stupor. I didn't have any one-size-fits-all answer for her, but I did offer to pray, so we bowed our heads over the phone and asked the Lord for His wisdom and His timing. "Lord, what do you want Vicki to do?"

Here it is that we find ourselves again, back at the question that's weaving its way throughout the whole of this book—a common thread of wonder, of doubt, and of sincere longing: Can a mom be creative in the midst of motherhood? And can this creative mother then turn her creativity into a business right there from the confines of her home, a business of art amidst the busyness of motherhood?

The answers to these questions are both simple and complicated. The simple answer is, of course! Women do this every day, living motherhood and art together in one long tangle of life. How this weaving together looks, however, is where it gets complicated, because it's different for each gifted woman. But the banner under which we all journey is surprisingly similar.

> Can a mom be creative in the midst of motherhood? And can this creative mother then turn her creativity into a business right there from the confines of her home, a business of art amidst the busyness of motherhood?

Hearing the Now

How do I know if now is the right time? How can I know if this will work? What if I fail, or worse, what if I fail my family? These are common questions women ask themselves as they begin the process of dream chasing. Failure. It's a fear that plagues us all when we prepare to step beyond the predictable routines of our motherly lives, and head into the more uncharted territory of working mom. What if my voice, my words, my images aren't good enough? What if I spend money to create something and don't earn any of it back? What if I have to be away from home more than I thought? What if I can't keep my records, and taxes are a mess, and I'm a mess too? What if? What if? What if?

It's not always as simple as listening for that still, small voice, is it? Though Ellie heard it crystal clear, and I prayed that my friend Vicki would too, sometimes God directs us in less conventional ways, without a tidy answer for each and every what if.

Several years ago, my husband and I packed up our home and our three young children, and we made a cross-country move from one state to another. Living on the coast had long been a dream of ours, and with our children still young enough to move easily, we decided the time was right to pursue settling in a place that we loved. We spent a lot of time praying over this decision, and as we prayed, opportunities for my husband's work opened up and the timing seemed right, so we began the process. Within a few months we had sold our home and were rolling down the highway . . . suddenly terrified that we'd made a *huge* mistake.

Thankfully we made a weeklong stop right in the middle of our cross-country adventure to visit with my husband's family. In those quiet days, we tried to wrap our minds around the huge, life-altering decision we'd just made. It felt so right at first, but as we said all our good-byes, that feeling of confirmation waned. My husband began to question everything. The new position he'd accepted suddenly felt like a terrible career move. Leaving the home where all of our children had been born seemed foolish and rash. He was overcome with anxiety, and I was overcome with anger, betrayed by what I perceived to be his change of heart.

It was here that the Lord met us through the calm, clear wisdom of my father-in-law.

We sat together in the bedroom, and my husband poured out his every fear while I sat fuming in the corner. We'd spoken for so long and this was what we'd agreed that we wanted for our family, and now it all felt wrong because of his doubts. I was angry and he was confused. Together we were a mess.

"I feel like I made the wrong decision, Dad," he said, choking back tears. "I'm afraid I've ruined my career, and I've uprooted my family for all the wrong reasons. I don't know what to do." My father-in-law listened quietly, as was his way, waiting until his son had laid bare every fear that threatened to crush his spirit.

"Son," he replied, his voice gentle, "you need to understand something about God and decision-making. You say you made the wrong decision, but the fact of the matter is that if you were seeking God in the process, and your desire was to follow Him, then the decision you made is the decision God *wanted* you to make."

"But I could have just as easily stayed put!" my husband said, throwing his hands up in exasperation. "We didn't *have* to move. What if I made the wrong choice?"

His father shook his head. "That's not the way God works. God isn't laying out options before you, trying to trick you into choosing the right path. You sought the Lord in this situation, and you made a decision. That's the decision He wanted you to make."

"But I never really heard a strong word from God that we were supposed to do this. I just sort of decided to do it. So how do I know I didn't choose what I wanted for myself? What if this isn't what God had for us?"

"You're missing the point, son." His voice grew firm, and I leaned in. "The point is, you made this decision; therefore, it's the decision God wanted you to make. If you had chosen to stay and not move away, then *that* would have been the decision God wanted you to make. God presented you with options, and they were both good options. You made a decision, and you can trust you made a good decision."

"What if it all goes wrong?" my husband asked.

My father-in-law smiled gently. "It could be tough, yes. But God will use that for your refinement. We can make decisions that result in uncomfortable consequences, but that doesn't make them wrong. This is all part of the grace He extends. But you need to hear me right now—God doesn't always give an audible sign as to where He wants you to go. Sometimes, you're going to have to just take a step forward and trust that your decision is under that umbrella of grace. He's going to take care of you."

Sometimes, you're going to have to just take a step forward.

Friends, you won't always be given a sign, or hear an audible direction about where you should go next, but this is not cause for fear or confusion. This is freedom! In looking to pursue a business out of your art, you may find yourself at a crossroads. Do you hit *publish* on your first blog post? Open up an Etsy shop full of graphic art? Sell your smocked little girl dresses to the shop downtown? Do you step forward and pursue your dreams today, or do you wait a little longer? While I can't give you the answers to those questions, I can encourage you to *evaluate* if pursuing a business endeavor is right for you at this time.

First, do you have a solid support system as you take these next steps? Do you have lifeguards who know you well and can honestly and graciously point you in the right direction, whether that be your husband or a small circle of business-savvy friends to help you navigate the course, or both?

Next, evaluate where you are with your children in this particular season. Honestly and realistically assess if you can handle the time it will take to build a business. I, for example, am a woman who has limits to how much she can take on. I know that I get easily overwhelmed, so I work to limit my yeses.

Other women are able to take on much more than I can, and they do so graciously and gracefully. Perhaps these women are in a different season of life, or maybe they have more help with the children. It's possible their personalities and hard wiring simply allow them to multitask with pizzazz, energized by the activity in ways that leave me exhausted. Whatever the case, the point is, what looks like a healthy work–life balance for me may be entirely different for someone else. This is another part of what makes us all so very unique in both ability and outreach.

So we fasted and petitioned our God about this, and he answered our prayer. (Ezra 8:23 NIV)

Finally, and most importantly, pray. It cannot be stressed enough from chapter to chapter that each desire and endeavor needs to be laid before the Lord. Seeking Him each day in those sanctified, drawn-away moments is the process by which all decision-making will find its natural, peaceful balance.

How will you know if now is the time to start a business of art in the busyness of motherhood? Have you bathed the process in prayer, have you received the support of your family, and do you feel confident you can handle the added load? If you have peace on these fronts, then it just might be the time to take that entrepreneurial step of faith. And as you sojourn, trusting in the Lord with each confident step forward, you just may find that the profit garnered from your surrendered yes is a blessing entirely unexpected.

Indeed, my friends, He is taking *such* good care of you.

Chapter Twelve

Renaissance Mom in a Digital Age

If the light that is on you is brighter than the light that is in you, the light that is on you will destroy you.

Christine Caine

A good playlist of music with a pot of hot tea is the fuel that keeps her going. Two all-nighters a month when it's time for a new project launch; it wouldn't work for me, but it does for Alle.

I searched the web over for a graphic designer to build my new blog. I'd imagined an analytical techie who would be open to my artistic sensibilities. Obviously, I knew nothing about the process of designing an online space, nor the marvelous artists who make this their career.

The name of her company sold me in just three words: *Finding Eden Media*. Before long we were emailing color swatches and textures back and forth. Hours and pages of in-depth questions helped us discover together what I most longed to communicate online. Needless to say, I was shocked by the exhaustive heart and soul, not to mention artistic flair, she poured into our project. *Our project.* I'd referred to it as mine at first, but when artists get together a miracle melding happens and no one can take complete ownership anymore.

Alle McCloskey's passion, I daresay her *mission*, is "to see the online conversation filled with the redemptive work of Jesus"—to guide creative people into their own personal Eden, because Alle believes in the breadth, width, and depth of influence that can be had in this digital age. And so she's made a career of helping others walk out their unique good works in the seemingly esoteric world of cyberspace. With her sweeping skill set, Alle fleshes out the unique callings of creative Christians, then builds, with technical artistry, a launching pad capable of reaching the farthest corners of the world.

All the while, Alle works daily to create an Eden for her two young boys within the Jerusalem of her home. As a natural offshoot of her devotion to those little men, she served for a time as brand manager for The MOB Society, an online community dedicated to Mothers of Boys. Her husband, Nate, is more than just her partner in life; he is also her business partner—likewise creative, technical, and entirely committed to infusing the virtual world with more of Jesus. It's the goal that drives their creative careers, and often keeps them up all night. However, since they *are* parents, they take turns on their all-nighters so that someone has the wherewithal to care joyfully for the boys come morning.

It was late on the night before my blog's launch when Alle walked me through all of my revamped social media sites. Facebook, YouTube, Twitter, Instagram, she'd tied them all together seamlessly with colors and fonts that would become my online signature. It was then, in the beauty of it all, that I felt a hollow pit in my stomach and began confessing all my fears. *Platform, likes, followers, fans*: those were the words that made my stomach lurch.

If you could hear a woman nod on the other end of a phone line, you would've heard Alle doing so in the silence. I finished speaking, and all my fear hung between us for a few long seconds before Alle asked if she could pray for me. More than an artist and professional—Alle had now become a minister to my anxious heart.

Doing Hard Things

Not every creative mom will start a business or ministry. God tells us in His Word that He knows the plans He has for us, that He's numbered our steps, and prepared specific good works for each of us to walk in. If launching a business isn't His plan for you, then praise Him for His clear voice. However, if you have offered up that surrendered yes and now feel His holy prompting to move out into the world in this way, the next couple of chapters are specifically for you.

This is where we get down and dirty, talking through two of the most awkward components of this Christian creative life—that of building a platform, and profiting from our art. This is the crossroad where art and ministry and business intersect.

There are great books available today on building your brand, garnering followers, finding your voice, knowing your audience, and utilizing Search Engine Optimization (SEO); this is not that kind of book. If you're looking for the nuts and bolts of platform building, I suggest you start with Michael Hyatt's popular resource, *Platform*. However, if the idea of having followers makes you just a bit nauseous at this point, then join me first in this conversation.

Why do we need a platform and how can we stay emotionally and spiritually healthy in the process?

If you're a visual artist, you need to hang that canvas on a wall or prop it up on your mantel to be seen. In your closet it will simply gather dust. Agreed? And if you want to share it with more than just your intimate family and friends, you need an Instagram or Flicker account. Simple. If you're a spoken word artist, rhythmically telling stories, you need a microphone, some sort of recording device, and a YouTube channel. It's necessary. Those of you with knitting needles, and scarves piled high, need a shop like Etsy, or a website of your own. Writers need a venue to find readers. And so on. Whether you're charging money for your creation or giving it away for free, the Internet is your storefront and your branding is the marketing that brings people in. You need a platform.

Only here's where the pit in my stomach (and maybe yours too) starts to ache: an online platform seems a whole lot like a stage with a spotlight shining directly on you. Many creatives are introverts to the core, so the imagery might make you quake a bit in your boots. Others of you are up-front personalities, more comfortable standing before an audience than alone in your room. Either way, we all need a healthy understanding of who we are and why we're ascending those platform steps, because it can be an awkward climb, especially when you're writing about, proclaiming, marketing your faith in Christ.

As we discussed a few chapters back, standing onstage can be dangerous for any artist, whether or not your art is directly related to ministry. Yes, even the baker of meringues, the designer of beaded handbags, and the home decorator shuffling furniture around a room are not immune to the lure of fame. It's here we remind ourselves that *whatever we do, in word or deed (or artistry), we do it all in the name of Jesus Christ.* That's our mantra, ladies. That's our goal. It's His fame and not our own we seek. So it's good and right to come to the Lord this way, trembling with healthy fear and trepidation because we do not long to build our own kingdom, but to build His. Not to increase our name but to lift high the Name above all names. Not basking in the spotlight but reflecting the Light out into the world.

> Whether you're charging money for your creation or giving it away for free, the Internet is your storefront and your branding is the marketing that brings people in. You need a platform.

Yes, we've spoken of humility before, but the truly humble still need a firm foundation upon which to stand. Quaking knees and all, you and I need a platform.

Drawing Attention

Each and every time my husband and I drive down the road and an old beater covered in bumper stickers pulls in front of us, my guy says, "I bet no one listened to that dude in junior high." Then he looks at me laughing. But I'm not laughing now, what with the gnawing in my gut, because I think that lots of people online today are just like that 1992 Corolla covered in bumper stickers, wanting so desperately to be heard.

Especially in this season confined to home, many creative women hunger to be part of the conversation—even if the conversation is just about slow-cooker dinners and DIY bows for their daughter's hair. So they invite themselves to the online party and attach bumper stickers to their cocktail dresses. "Listen to me, I've got something to say!" Similarly, here I sit, filling up a book with my opinions on things no one asked me for . . . and I have to say it's awkward. Like throwing oneself into the ether in a sticker-covered dress.

Beep Beep. Look at me!

However, for the Christian creative it's more than a simple desire to be heard, more than creativity longing for sweet release. It's a red-hot burning in our bones that begs to get out and start a wildfire. We aren't passive participants at this Renaissance Faire, but are actively involved in a modern-day revival online—creatively leading people to embrace life and faith.

Beep Beep. Look at Him!

While self-indulgence tempts us all, I'd venture to say that many of you reading this book are fighting it, as am I. Still, creativity just sort of bubbles up and out like a natural geyser. And as it flows from my own life, I pray that what shoots heavenward is at least water—hopefully Living Water—and not just hot air. Water flowing up and out and getting readers, customers, audience members soaked through. A baptism of beauty. That's my ultimate desire. That's why I dare step upon that platform, awkward as it may be. That's why you blog. That's why you sing. That's why you put your notecards with swirling Scriptures up on your Etsy site. And that's why I drive our family Suburban covered in Jesus stickers, because I'm passionate about the Living Water.

Beep Beep. Look at Him!

There are people I know and love who aren't impressed. They judge my motives as I stand upon my platform, and criticize my bumper-sticker style, but I've decided that will have to be all right. It's got to be, because the natural push to communicate online God's radical nearness in my everyday life is stronger than my need to please them. There are, however, times I leave my sticker-laden car in the garage because I'm just so tired—not of the writing or the painting or the sharing but of the awkwardness of the platform and the way it continues to threaten my balance, makes me check to see how many people "like" me or how many "fans" I have.

Beep Beep. Look at Him!

The honking of the horn shakes me loose. Look at Him. Look at Him. The whole idea of the Christian platform is summed up in those three words: look at Him.

Maintaining Authenticity

Nicole Johnson is a wife, mother, and the dramatist for Women of Faith. But there's more to her story than the sanctified season she spent away from her work so that she might be fully present with her growing family. And so it was that as Nicole and I met up one afternoon, she offered her wisdom in other areas of this creative life.

At one point in our conversation, I asked how she keeps her head straight when there's a mile-long line of women waiting to hug her neck and buy a book after one conference, and at the next location it's like a ghost town at her table as everyone circles around Lucy Swindoll or Steven Curtis Chapman. She laughed like it was an absurd question, but her eyes told of the struggle that taught her wisdom. "There will be critics," she said. "There will always be plenty of women who don't like my costume or my accent, or maybe my story just didn't resonate. Other nights, however, it does resonate for lots of people, and they stand in line to tell me, which of course feels good. But if I get caught up in the praise, or need their affirmation after every performance, I will get lost." She paused for a moment, and I let her words sink in. "I've learned that all I'm responsible for is getting up there and doing my job the best I can," she continued, "so when I step off the platform it's His whisper I listen for. *Well done.*"

"Speaking of platforms . . ." I broached the subject tentatively. "What about online? Do you ever get caught up in the numbers game on Instagram or YouTube?"

Again the laughter, and again the wisdom. "Listen, if I can't do Instagram authentically, I can't do Instagram." I thought of my own journey online and the moments I felt pressured to be funny and quirky, or deeply spiritual for the purpose of engaging with my online "friends" in order to appear relevant and present. Those are the days I lose sight of who my bedrock is, and think more about the height and the sparkly goodness of the platform I'm building. Those are also the days I struggle most as a mom—days when I'm concerned about the number of likes or comments or sales or shares. Nicole broke through my quiet convictions with these words: "The fact that I'm not online all the time may not be what my book publisher wants for me, but if they want me, then they get authentic me."

> Tweeting, re-tweeting, scoping, sharing, liking, tagging, inviting . . . If I can't do it authentically, then I can't do it.

Let me repeat the idea again, because these words have become the litmus test for everything I do online: if I can't do it authentically, then I can't do it.

Tweeting, re-tweeting, scoping, sharing, liking, tagging, inviting . . . if I can't do it authentically, then I can't do it. Likewise, if I can't manage to engage in the online conversation without snapping at my children, missing out on our family time at home, and forsaking my husband in the evenings to communicate with my online people, then that's a problem too.

All that said, some women are doing this online Renaissance exceptionally well. So well, in fact, I think God may have masterminded the whole world of social media for His own glory.

Where People Gather

The first time I stumbled across one of her photos, I gasped. Literally gasped. It was all right there, faith and art intersected in the most worshipful of ways. I didn't really expect to find God on Instagram, not wrapped up in such fresh creativity, but there He was. His Words brought to life, then captured and shared for my encouragement.

> Bless the LORD, O my soul!
> O LORD my God, You are very great;
> You are clothed with splendor and majesty,
> Covering Yourself with light as with a cloak,
> Stretching out heaven like a tent curtain.
> He lays the beams of His upper chambers in the waters;
> He makes the clouds His chariot;
> He walks upon the wings of the wind. (Ps. 104:1–3)

This passage of Scripture is beautiful all on its own. God-breathed poetry. However, the picture posted on Instagram took the verses to a new level of beauty. Utilizing colored pencils and her artist's eye, Shanna Noel drew a masculine hand over the words of her Bible. As God's fingers gently guided swirling waters across the page, Shanna drew us deeper into this Scripture than I had ever gone before. Right there on Instagram, in front of God and everybody, a personal faith was illustrated, uploaded, and shared with the world.

When this Renaissance mom of two young girls first began illustrating her faith, she did so as a form of private worship. Right there in the pages of her journaling Bible, the Word came alive as she offered her drawing and scrapbooking skills back to the One who made her so creative. Shortly after, at the start of 2014, Shanna heard a whisper. "This is meant to be shared." Hesitant, she kept up her creative worship in the quiet of her own home until one day she felt a clear, strong push to snap a photo.

That one post on Instagram ignited a wildfire as creative women everywhere reached out and excitedly affirmed this beautiful new form of worship. Within months, the Illustrated Faith movement took off and Shanna found herself at the helm, encouraging and equipping women to not just read the words in their Bible but to really explore them. Using simple tools from the scrapbooking industry, the Illustrated Faith community took to Instagram and Facebook, inspiring thousands of women to pursue a deeper knowledge of God through His Word.

Years ago, Shanna's gift would have likely been confined to her family's enjoyment, a legacy passed down to grandchildren and great-grandchildren perhaps. Possibly she could have blessed her local church or women's ministry with her skill set too. Today, however, it's ignited a worldwide phenomenon, a revival so to speak, thanks to the digital age. One woman's faith, filtered through the lens of her unique abilities, then shared authentically in the online realm of social media.

> When creative talent and gospel love collide with the power of the Internet, a tidal wave of impact flows far beyond our reach.

When creative talent and gospel love collide with the power of the Internet, a tidal wave of impact flows far beyond our reach. This is the effect of social media, flowing out from a creative's heart to the ends of the earth, a visual wildfire of gospel-infused artistry.

city gates (*noun*). The place where people gather, conversations are spoken, goods are purchased, the sick are brought for healing, and people offer up their praises.

In ancient civilizations, Israel included, elders from the land met together at their city gates. There they sat sharing wisdom, judging conflicts, and speaking of the Lord together. Boaz was known to sit at the city gates, as was the husband of the Proverbs 31 woman. Moses, Joshua, Samuel, and Ezekiel all mentioned the importance of these gates and those gatherings, and King Solomon reminded us multiple times that wisdom herself cries out at the gates of our city.

Does not wisdom call,
And understanding lift up her voice?
On top of the heights beside the way,
Where the paths meet, she takes her stand;
Beside the gates, at the opening to the city,
At the entrance of the doors, she cries out. (Prov. 8:1–3)

While those were ancient times, and this digital age is thoroughly modern, the reality remains the same: those who have something to say must go to where the people gather, and today women are gathering together online. In this digital age, Facebook is one of the many gates where we sit and discuss what is most important to us, where we sell our goods and lend our voices and upload our images.

People are gathering, with multiple generations coming together online, and a dialogue has begun. There's a melding happening, where those who create and share their words and their wares are stepping into ministry positions at these metaphorical gates. If you're one of those reaching people via your giftedness on the World Wide Web, if your artistry allows you to live out your faith in an authentic light-shining way, then you are His minister, creatively ministering from your home, out into the world.

Give her the product of her hands,
And let her works praise her in the gates. (Prov. 31:31)

The truth of the matter is that your voice in this digital conversation has eternal significance, as everything you do online is an opportunity to let your light shine publicly. From the pictures of your children's birthday parties and the recipes you share, to your DIY projects and the tutus you make!

Come boldly and with purpose, embracing your giftedness. Bring it to the Lord, who is our sure foundation, and ask Him to build with you a platform in the midst of this special season in your family's life. Come and lend your voice to the conversation.

When my husband and I were first married, we went to the new members class at our church. One of the getting-to-know-you questions we answered aloud as a group was, how did you come to know Christ? Out of fifteen people, three of them said, "I was invited to the Christmas play." Every year this church would put on a Christmas spectacular that included singing and a storyline, and always concluded in the gospel message. Today, only a decade later, that same church discontinued this fruitful Christmas play. Why? Because their local community stopped coming. In just a handful of years, people began looking elsewhere for their answers and entertainment. I believe that they've turned to the Internet for both. It's there, in that online sphere, that Christian creatives just like you shine their lights from a different sort of stage.

It's so bright, I dare say, that if I were the devil I'd get pretty upset. Social media has been one of his favorite domains this past decade, and he doesn't want you in it. That's a fiery fact, so be on your guard. He plots from without and within, ensnaring with the lure of Christian fame, ministry prosperity, and platform popularity, and it doesn't take him long to tempt even the purest heart. This temptation is one of the devil's favorite ploys, no different than what church leaders around the world have experienced throughout history, as he tries to keep the focus on numbers instead of souls.

> If you stand upon a platform as a follower of Christ, you make yourself an open target for the enemy's flaming arrows.

And so he leans in close and whispers, "I'll keep them busy with their platform, so that they forget the One they intended to place upon it. I will keep them blinded behind their megaphone, that they lose sight of their message. I will tickle their hearts when people 'like' their fan page, and big churches invite them to lead worship. And I will whisper lies when people don't leave comments, or share their graphics. I will make them question if they belong upon that stage. Oh, what a field day I'll have. In the end, they will become bitter and embarrassed and leave this realm again to me."

My friends, doesn't that make you shiver? I know you didn't sign up for this. But this is the war we're in. If you stand upon a platform as a follower of Christ, you make yourself an open target for the enemy's flaming arrows. Therefore, as you build the scaffolding beneath the stage, build it strong and secure. Abide securely in the Cornerstone, and know your message, for He's the one who created you creative. Surround yourself with like-minded friends and family members, those lifeguards who will help remind you of your calling when your knees buckle and your feet of clay begin to slide.

Take courage, creative women, though you may find yourself a bit clumsy as you climb the platform stairs. Take courage, and join the conversation, willing to be seen and heard.

Chapter Thirteen

When Art Turns a Profit

> God didn't equip us with unique talents, insights, drives, and ambitions for us to be ashamed of them. He meant us to use those to serve others in the marketplace. And people are waiting for what you have to offer.
>
> Michael Hyatt

In June 2005, three men launched a little website with a nonsense name. The idea was to build a brand from scratch, and to change the way sellers did business online. They were on the cutting edge of a new trend.

Sell what you make, and make what you sell.

Etsy was unique in that it offered crafters the opportunity to sell their art in the comfort of their own homes. Gone were the days when the crafting genius had to peddle her product in local boutiques, or enter into every craft fair within a fifty-mile radius to get her art to the world. Now she could market it from her living room.

Taking the site to a new level, Etsy added the vintage component, capitalizing on the up-and-coming phenomenon of refurbishing and selling antique pieces. Shabby chic was chic, and with a can of paint and the flip of a wrist, we could be too. With the launch, and the subsequent marketing developments, Etsy singlehandedly opened up a whole new realm in this online Renaissance.

> In this modern-day Renaissance, the guest room closet becomes the center of operations, and the crafty mom with a surrendered yes now has the potential to own her own business.

For the creative mom pouring her energy into her home, sites like Etsy open up a world of possibilities. Suddenly the sewing machine in the corner is more than another place to store junk—it's now an opportunity. In this modern-day Renaissance, the guest room closet becomes the center of operations, and the crafty mom with a surrendered yes now has the potential to own her own business. But owning a business comes with a price. It takes time and research, dedication and commitment, and often a little capital. There are logistics to be figured out in order to run a successful business from home, but the joy of making a successful go of it can be thrilling.

> She makes linen garments and sells them,
> And supplies belts to the tradesmen. (Prov. 31:24)

Producing a profit for your work is a unique privilege, especially in this day and age when you can work from home with your children by your side. Gone are the days when the only choice for mom was stay at home or work outside the home. Today the sky's the limit, and your own imagination sits firmly in the pilot's seat. The potential to earn a wage from your living room table is an important component of this Renaissance age.

Like two friends meeting in a coffee shop—though actually Skyping through the computer screen after all the children had been tucked into bed—we sat face-to-face and talked about motherhood, faith, and creativity. It was a delight to interact on a more personal level because, you see, I felt like I already knew her.

I'd come to know Darlene Weir, the master designer behind the wildly successful interior design business, Fieldstone Hill, through that same thirteen-inch screen. I'd seen her heart and her art showcased in beautiful photographs via her social media channels, and watched as she decorated rooms, brought kitchen nooks to life, and transformed walls from bare to vibrant thanks to her artistic touch and attention to detail. I was so inspired I even patterned my living room décor after her signature style.

Beyond her inspiring decorating photos, I found equal delight in the pictures Darlene posted of her growing family: two older boys, bustling with energy, and her newest addition, a baby girl with plump, rosy cheeks, and a giant bow—always a bow.

It was a year and a half after the birth of her daughter that Darlene and I "met," leaning into our computer screens and talking late into the night. We both nodded our way through the conversation, and would have reached in and clasped each other's hands if technology had allowed. At some points we were loud as schoolgirls, and at other moments we spoke in hushed, hallowed tones, like when Darlene told me how she was reemerging from those harried months with a new baby. It was the tail end of a time when she'd placed her career on the back burner so that she could focus on the changing dynamics of her growing family. Stepping away from exciting opportunities and the profitability of her successful business hadn't been easy, but she knew it was a necessary sacrifice.

"It was hard," she told me. "But I had to say no to some wonderful opportunities for a time and accept the fact that my creative gifts weren't going away. And neither was my creative business." As we continued our conversation, Darlene and I went deep into our common passion for art and business, and the glorious coupling of the two in the midst of motherhood. It was here that Darlene confessed how she once struggled with the concept of what it might look like to blend faith into the mix of a successful interior design business.

"I looked at other successful bloggers, and I found myself comparing what I did to what they were doing, as though maybe my efforts, and the end results of those efforts, weren't worthy enough. These were women raising funds for adoption and charities, while I worked for a paycheck. I really had to wrestle through that before I could move forward." Darlene's voice trailed off. There was a long pause as she carefully chose her next words. "In my wrestling, I realized that at the core of my struggle to monetize my work is the fact that most of us tend to devalue our art as though it's not enough. We convince ourselves it needs to be something more. *We* need to be something more. More talented . . . more spiritual . . ." Her voice trembled just slightly. "And maybe this isn't just a problem for creative women, but for *all* women. How often do we downplay our contribution to the world around us?"

I nodded when she strung those words together because I could identify with the struggle that she presented. And maybe you can too.

A Valuable Contribution

Art is a valuable thing. Collectors of great masterpieces have bet their wealth on it, and if this is true, then we can naturally deduce that artists are valuable as well. We create beauty in a world that often feels ugly. When fires burn and terrorism reigns, we bring the healing light of hope through our artistic contributions.

Art is valuable; therefore, artists are valuable too.

> Art is valuable; therefore, artists are valuable too.

Before we even talk about price tags and profit, let's just grapple with this core component—we have something of worth to contribute to this world. Whether you create simply as an overflow and give your creations away freely, or you create with a longing to profit from your art, you, dear mom, bring value to this world. Rejoice in that! Yet for some reason as creatives, particularly creative women, we're quick to shrug our shoulders and dismiss these gifts as frivolous, thereby undervaluing them before we even open shop. In this age that idolizes big platforms, bright lights, Internet fame, and viral success, these feelings of inadequacy lead us to question our small place in the online marketplace, and our worthiness to make a profit.

Dear creative friends, this must not be the case! You are a steward of talents. You may be familiar with the parable of the talents in Matthew 25:14–30, where one servant is given one talent, another two, and another five—according to their abilities. Knowing that their master is a hard man, the first servant buries his coin in the sand, so that he doesn't lose it. The man with two talents invests his money wisely and makes an impressive return. And the servant entrusted with five talents yields his master five more, due to his shrewd stewardship. Of course Jesus is talking about talents, as in coins, but we're talking about artistic talents too, because isn't everything He gives us ours to steward wisely for the greatest return? So all of this leads me to ask: What will you do with what the Master has entrusted to you?

> Attaching value to the hours you spend laboring over each handmade treasure isn't unbiblical for the creative Christian.

Bury it?

Invest it?

Use it?

Charge for it?

Give it away?

Regardless of the choice you make, the gifts you possess, along with the hours in your day, are entirely yours to steward, so steward them well. If you've offered your dreams back to the Lord, and you've given Him your surrendered yes to follow where He leads, then the banner of His grace now rests upon each decision you make. And if you long to make a profit from your art, then this is what I want you to take away: attaching value to the hours you spend laboring over each handmade treasure isn't unbiblical for the creative Christian.

In all labor there is profit,
But mere talk leads only to poverty. (Prov. 14:23)

Pressing the telephone to my ear, I stepped into the closet to muffle out the happy sounds of my children in the next room. Her voice was weak and shaky, like a woman under attack. She spoke of her love for the written word, how she wrote a book to encourage and exhort, of the care and prayers she poured out on pages—the book that she wanted to give away for *free* until a friend pulled her aside and urged her to charge for it.

"I feel uncomfortable placing a price on these words because they're prayerful words, and I meant for them to bless women, not bless me! Besides, wouldn't putting a price on this message about the gift of God's grace be backward and wrong? His grace was given *freely* to me . . . so shouldn't I give this message away for free?"

I hung my head in empathy. Many times over I've heard women say that profiting from their artistic work is difficult, especially when the art is Christian in nature: songs, books, Scripture prints, and one-woman shows produced for women's events and conferences. "I feel as though I'm peddling the gospel," she continued, "and it all feels so wrong." Then her voice just trailed off.

I cut through the brief silence, filling the void with my own uncomfortable questions: "Why do we do that? Why do women, especially creative Christian women, feel guilt for profiting from the hundreds, if not thousands, of hours we've labored? What is it about turning a profit that scares us?"

We both got quiet as we pondered the questions, and when the phone call was over I continued to let this inquiry simmer.

Believing Your Worth

We have no control over the gifts and talents given to us, but we have every responsibility for their stewardship.

Erwin Raphael McManus

When she picks up a camera, you see it happen; her entire demeanor changes. Her face lights up, and her hands move quickly through the motions as she adjusts settings. Shielding her eyes, she glances up at the sky then looks around, taking in her surroundings. The artist is at work, and you sense that she's catching the vision before she's even snapped a picture.

My dear friend Tammy is the visionary behind Tammy Labuda Photography. She's not just uniquely skilled with a camera, but she's also deftly gifted at editing photos, so much so that each picture she takes becomes an heirloom-quality masterpiece. Tammy tells a story each time the shutter clicks.

In an era where anyone with an iPhone can capture meaningful moments, Tammy has taken steps to rise above the throng, constantly honing her skill through study. She attends seminars and downloads courses. She takes classes from those who are more skilled than she is, and gleans from their expertise. And with all the time and energy that Tammy has poured into mastering her art, it only makes sense that she should charge according to her ability.

Tammy and I spoke at length that summer day after she finished taking photos of my family. We dove together into this uncomfortable topic of business, and talents, and profit, and the process of crossing the line from creative hobby to full-blown business. I listened as her voice rose, and her cheeks grew red. It wasn't anger that got her so worked up, but passion. Tammy is passionate about capturing the intrinsic value in each of her client's portraits, but she also wants to honor and steward her craft well.

"I believe that I offer a legitimate service and a tangible product that should be purchased at what the industry says it's worth—not just to compensate me, but to protect my fellow photographers and the industry as a whole," Tammy told me as she carefully put her camera away that afternoon.

"If I give my work away for free, it undermines those who have to charge just to put food on the table. It makes it harder for them to survive. Getting paid doesn't make me feel more valued as a person, but it does help my sense of self-worth to know that I'm 'playing fair' and being a better steward of my time, resources, and talents." She sat back and looked at me thoughtfully before continuing.

"I work hard so that I can bless other families, but I want to bless my own family too," she said. "I spend hours doing what I do because I want to offer back the very best that I can to my clients. And my very best takes time, which I have to guard because that's time that takes away from being with my husband and children. Getting paid doesn't give me that time back, but it adds a different sort of value to my family. I lose the time with them, but we also gain so much in return. When I'm working hard, I feel fulfilled in my calling. The additional finances relieve my husband of some of the financial burden. And most importantly, my children witness firsthand what it means to work well with others, and run an honest and successful business."

And there it is once again, the grace stretched out like a carpet upon this Renaissance path.

When you use your gifts to make a product, it is good to make a profit. I think of the question that my writer friend wrestled with, and of Tammy's business-savvy wisdom, and I see how it all swirls together. And what I've discovered is this: what you do adds *value* to this world, whether it's creative work with photo editing software, or penning grace-filled words in the dark

> When you use your gifts to make a product, it is good to make a profit.

hours of the night. Both of these offerings are valuable, and monetizing your skill can be part of the stewardship process, if that is what you long to do.

You're doing a real job, and there are bills to pay. A price tag tied on the end of the hours you spent creating says, "This job of mine, this message, this canvas, this frame . . . holds worth." Your art is the culmination of long labor, and "the laborer is worthy of his wages" (1 Tim. 5:18).

Several years ago as I began ramping up my career as a writer and editor, I took on a lot of jobs without pay. I rationalized this choice by convincing myself that I needed to build a name for myself, and show that I had experience. But as the work took off it became a lot to manage, and suddenly I found myself stressed over everything. That's when my husband pulled me aside one evening after the kids were tucked into bed.

"You need to stop working for free," he told me as we sat nestled on our wicker couch on the front porch, enjoying the cool, September air. "If you don't value your time and skill, the people you're working for won't either." I tried to defend my reasoning for offering free services, but he stopped me, and I knew it was time to listen. My husband is a successful businessman. I needed to hear his words and ingest them.

"I know that you're gifted," he said. "I know that you're good at what you do. In fact, lots of people know it. But it's time that *you believe* that you're good enough to start charging for it." That was a turning point for me professionally, but it wasn't easy to retrain my thoughts. I was fearful that I would lose opportunity if I started charging, and I did on occasion. Some people simply couldn't afford to pay me, and I had to walk away from those projects. But the people who *were* willing to pay agreed with the value I had placed on my time and skill, and I found that working with the promise of compensation gave me more confidence, thereby eliminating much of my stress, which in turn relieved some of the burden and stress from my family who had to live with me.

Friends, God has given you talents, and with them may come the opportunity to produce a financial blessing. Undervaluing the work that you do isn't His desire, nor does He ask us to hide timidly in the shadows as we meekly hold our wares out to a waiting world. Instead, He invites us to work hard and to charge for our services. We are living in a day and age when a mother's art can quite feasibly be turned into a business from the confines of her home. This is part of the grand blessing of living in this digital Renaissance, showcasing your talent within an appreciative marketplace, and yielding a financial return.

Or is He speaking altogether for our sake? Yes, for our sake it was written, because the plowman ought to plow in hope, and the thresher to thresh in hope of sharing the crops. If we sowed spiritual things in you, is it too much if we reap material things from you? (1 Cor. 9:10–11)

This value is found in every area of art, from the sacred to the secular. My friend Tammy found peace in working for a wage, as did I eventually, but what of my friend wrestling with whether or not to charge for her book? What of the woman working inside the church, using her artistic abilities to share God's Word with the world? Is it safe even there to garner a profit? The short answer is, most certainly! Yes, even for the person whose foremost spiritual gift is that of a Bible teacher, profiting from the message that's all wrapped in art is good and fair.

The Discipline of Business

I know that there is nothing better for them than to rejoice and to do good in one's lifetime; moreover, that every man who eats and drinks sees good in all his labor—it is the gift of God. (Eccl. 3:12–13)

All of this is good encouragement, but what does it really mean, and how do we put this into practice? Placing value on a service can be a difficult task, because who measures the worth of an artistic offering? We see value in the more tangible offerings of the business world, but when it comes to art, suddenly value is subjective. This is why we must practice the *discipline* of business alongside the discipline of creativity.

There's a great term used in the entertainment industry: *show business*. Those two words hold equal measure. To succeed, you must practice the *show,* and also practice the *business*. This translates well into any creative business venture. Increasing our ability to earn a wage requires that we regularly hone both the show (our creativity) and the business (marketing our art for sale). *Both* disciplines are required for our Christ-centered creativity to make its way up out of Jerusalem and into the world.

Writers must practice their writing, line after line, but also must work to connect with influencers inside their field; photographers practice the settings of their camera in the rising and the setting sun, but also study photo editing and pricing models; bakers practice their pie crust with the crumble on top, then closely observe how to market and sell their edible creations in the local marketplace.

Much of your business in the early stages will be researching what others in this Renaissance age are doing. Glean from those artists selling their watercolors and seamstresses their tablecloths. Learn from the decorators transforming homes, speakers sharing their gift at the podium, and painters offering their personalized canvases. Who are they, and what value have they placed on their offering? You'll start to see fees in a whole new light as you study their example. This is the business side of show business. This is the business side of a home decorating business. This is the business side of a culinary business. This is the business side of any business. And you can make it *your* business.

There's more to this equation than simply practicing, though. Finding your value within the marketplace requires an honest assessment of your skill level. You need to hold what you do up to the light of what others are doing in your field, and make a determination of where you fit on the scale of marketability.

Perhaps you need someone to help you figure this out, someone who can more objectively look at your current skill set within the marketplace, and help you set a fair price. Once you've determined where you fall on this scale, set your prices accordingly and walk confidently in that decision. This isn't the time to struggle with pride, for you've already accepted your skill as the gift that it is. Nor is this a time for insecurity, because true humility holds high her head knowing full well that God holds her worth. Accept this worth, and walk forward unashamed.

> If one advances confidently in the direction of his dreams, and endeavors to live the life which he has imagined, he will meet with a success unexpected in common hours.
>
> Henry David Thoreau, 1854

Profit in the Toil

It's the way you wrap a package, the way you tie a ribbon. Working that bow like a farmer works his soil until it gives up fruit that nourishes a community. Peaches sweet and apples crisp. Wheat tall and sun grown, made into the bread we break together. Your creative gifts are nourishing and life sustaining, much like that of the farmer, purposed for the good of your greater community.

However, these goods will never make their way into the hands of the people if you don't formulate a plan. A business plan. Generating a profitable income from your art doesn't just happen. It takes effort, even more sacrifice, and always a whole lot of perseverance. There will be obstacles on the path toward your dream of producing marketable art, and you need a plan set in place for conquering those obstacles.

The biggest roadblock in the path toward marketing our wares is simply understanding *how*. As you dedicate yourself to the discipline of turning your art into a profitable business, you'll find that there's plenty to keep you busy. You'll need to learn the ins and outs of running a business. How do you handle the finances? Do you incorporate, and if so, how do you do so? You need to prepare to file taxes, learn bookkeeping, and do many other tedious but necessary tasks. These things can be daunting, so seek out advisors. Your husband, a friend, a banker, parent, or online acquaintance whom you admire. Research takes work, and work takes time, so learn to manage your time accordingly.

It all sounds terribly overwhelming, doesn't it—this leaning into the work so that you can profit from the art? You see other women doing what you want to do, and they seem so flawless in their day-to-day operations, but as a wise friend told me one afternoon as we walked along the beach, "People make assumptions based only on what they see online. They don't know the sacrifice it took to get there."

It's true that a cursory glance at my friend's résumé makes it seem as though her life is perfectly balanced in her steady work as a designer while also managing three children under age eight. But as her career took off, she and her husband took some time to evaluate her opportunity, and they decided as a team to bring in help so that she could more easily manage her work and her family.

Once a month someone comes over and cleans her home, freeing up time to enjoy her family when she's not working. And twice a week a babysitter comes to the house and plays with the children while she heads to work. These are financial choices that my friend and her husband agreed on together, giving her the chance to fully develop as both a creative and a business owner.

What looks like "balance" for one mom from the outside looking in is really an intricately designed plan created to get through the busy days of life—*her* life. But let's face it: perfect balance is a myth. Finding complete balance is a bit like hunting for a unicorn. Maybe it's out there, but nobody has ever actually seen it; they've only heard that it exists.

The fact is, some of your days will be consumed with laundry piles and errands, while other days you abandon the stack of dishes in your sink to play with your children. Balance? Maybe if you step back far enough and squint your eyes real tight. But if you're looking for this elusive dream of balance in each and every mothering day, you'll be sorely disappointed.

When we dare throw the concept of balance out the window, we discover a world of freedom and not condemnation. The entrepreneurial beat of your heart will be free to find its own rhythm when it no longer feels wrapped in the need to live a balanced life. And your mothering heart will be free to indulge in long afternoons languishing poolside on a "work day"—because balance is a *myth*. So loosen the reins a bit as dreams and loved ones press in against your heart. Don't get caught up in a hunt for that which cannot be found in every twenty-four-hour span. Simply dedicate yourself to walking in your good works each day, one step at a time, one foot in front of the other, motherhood and business, and all the details that merge to make the two work in tandem.

I want nothing more than to leave you with the confidence that there is no wrong in valuing your art and your time. You can believe your gifts worthy of making a profit, if that's what you so desire. The key is in not fearing the process. Practice the discipline of business while giving yourself to the creative inspiration of art; and as the two begin to weave themselves together, walk steadily onto the Renaissance path before you.

Chapter Fourteen

Renaissance Rising

> Our children's gifts are sometimes buried deep.
> It's up to us to mine the gift in them, extract it,
> and allow it to be shaped and polished to be
> useful in building the kingdom of God.
>
> Kate Battistelli

They wrapped up their homeschool day early then loaded into the minivan. Kris Camealy hauled her four children to every Hobby Lobby, Michael's, and Target in a sixty-mile radius, scouring the shelves for paints and stamps, colored pencils and scrapbooking paper. This errand was the very last item on her long to-do list.

The following weekend, women traveled from all over to Salt Fork Lodge at the entrance of Ohio State Park, leaving their families behind for three days of rest and worship. Kris was the hostess who had imagined this retreat and christened the gathering *Refine*, prayerful that this wouldn't be just another conference where women heard from women, but an opportunity to truly retreat, pull away, and hear from the Lord in the natural splendor of His creation.

At the end of the lodge's long hallway sat an intimate conference room with large windows overlooking deep green oaks. A sign hung upon the door: *Art Journaling*. The length of the space was lined with tables covered in art supplies that tiny fingers had unearthed from dollar bins and clearance racks. From early morning till late at night, this room was open and available to the women.

Kris joined the happy throng who came to the creative sanctuary and eagerly waited for their leader to give instructions that first day. Surprisingly only one, simple charge was given: "Let the Lord move you. Let Him show you how to create."

While most of these women would call themselves creative in one way or another, few would label themselves visual artists. They looked at one another timidly at first, and at the blank journals and art supplies spread out before them like the sacrament of Holy Communion. Then slowly, in the quiet of their creative space, each one bravely touched pigment to paper.

It's an odd thing to take the walls off of worship and let it flow in new ways, celebrating Him through the expression of our in-His-image creativity. *Imago Dei.* Painting isn't our normal fare of worship. Worship is predictable. Worship is hymns that are familiar, and praying with heads bowed. Worship is what happens in church sanctuaries or at the kitchen table over coffee and God's Word before the rest of the family stirs. All of *that* is worship.

But taking the lid off a can of paint? Well, my friend, that's worship too. *Adovah worship.*

> When you are in high school, you don't give much thought to what you can't do. For most people, that gets learned later, and for still fewer, gets unlearned for the rest of life.
>
> Bob Goff

Have you ever noticed how a toddler's greedy little hands blend colors that clash, all while singing their songs off-key with complete abandon? Children live their worshipful lives unabashedly, unapologetically, and totally unaware that there might be some kind of formula. If we would take the time to sit down and really watch them, to observe their unbounded joy in all of life, we just might learn a thing or two about worship . . . and art.

But you and me, we're all grown up. We like to polish and perfect each painting, master and manipulate every message before we lift it up to Him. We are purposeful and they are playful. We are cerebral while our children are celestial, zealous in their self-expression. While we hum politely in the corner, they stand up on a picnic table and belt out "The B-I-B-L-E" with absolute joy! Theirs is the Renaissance rising, refreshing and responsive, and we've so much to glean from their example. Of course, they've also got much to learn from us and isn't that what family looks like—everyone learning together?

So it was for Kris and her children. On Sunday afternoon as the conference wound down, and the women packed up their hearts and arts, she loaded up the leftover supplies, along with exactly four unused art journals.

Four.

She made it home late that night, long after the kids were sleeping. In the morning when they reunited in the kitchen, she greeted them with squeals and kisses and gifts—an art journal for each one and a bin full of leftover supplies to share. Immediately they dove in as Kris turned to scrambling eggs and frying bacon. Unlike the women at *Refine*, Kris's children needed no prompting, no direction; they knew instinctively, intuitively, what to do with watercolors and oil pastels.

> We are purposeful and they are playful. We are cerebral while our children are celestial.

Kris told me the story of how she'd introduced art to her brood, only to have them introduce her to the art of diving in. We talked it through that day in May, as the peonies bloomed and her children colored with sidewalk chalk beyond the screen door. And I couldn't help but think of how hard it all is to bring our children into this messy creative life. But really it should be one of the most natural ways creative women connect with our children, when they're young and expressive, unhindered by perfectionism. Together over a palette of paint, or on the couch with an instrument cradled in the arms of each child, we teach them out of the *surplus* supplies of our own passionate pursuits. Better yet, the art naturally overflows from us onto them! Yes, we teach them from the overflow, and then watch how they teach us right back.

Parenting from the Overflow

When we fill our home with music that moves us, and an easel in the sun-drenched kitchen nook, not only are we constantly inspired, but our children have the opportunity to grow into inspired people too. As they watch us use our gifts in the local church to edify and encourage, they receive the overflowing example of gospel-centered creativity and mission-minded art.

All this sounds lovely, of course, except more often than not we don't bring them with us into our art, because it's all quite messy. So we set our art aside for this season with little ones at home, or use it as a holy time to pull away alone. But what if, instead of hording it up for our own self-expression, we shared with them the leftover art supplies and bathed them in the overflow? What if here, as we draw near the end of this book, we turn our gaze from our own present Renaissance, to fix our attention on the Renaissance rising?

Within my home live two wildly creative children. One is a master designer who keeps an arsenal of scotch tape in both his bedside table and top desk drawer. He wasn't a day over four when he emerged from his room one morning stark naked, except for the invisible tape and craft feathers that had transformed him into a bird. Another day I heard the high-pitched screech of the dispenser announcing the end of yet another roll, and my child came out of his room with a pen strapped to each knuckle; he was Wolverine. The afternoon that he spray-painted cardboard boxes silver and duct-taped them together in the form of a robot costume let me know just how deeply his creativity was rooted. There he was, all bound up in craft supplies, crying big, wet tears . . . heartbroken that his costume didn't magically transform him into a real live robot. His pain was visceral.

His brother is a musician, fingers flying over strings, a harmonica strapped to his mouth, finding chords no one has taught him. He is twelve and homeschooled so that he might have the time he needs each day to explore his unique giftedness. Half-way through math, when the numbers can't find their rhythm, I send him to the garage to play. He picks up his iPad, searching for a new song, and learns it

> While I am part of today's Renaissance, I am intensely aware of the next one rising just down the hall.

in an afternoon. Before calling him back to his math, I take a video and send it to my husband who hurries home to pick up his own guitar and play with his son.

While I am part of today's Renaissance, I am intensely aware of the next one rising just down the hall.

"Have you met Kate?" asked my friend. Before I could answer, she reached out and caught hold of the woman casually passing by.

"Kate?" I asked.

"Kate Battistelli," she said as an introduction, extending her hand to me with a smile.

And thus began another one of the amazing friendships sprouted in the fertile soil of a conference room.

"Battistelli . . . are you related to the singer Francesca Battistelli?" I asked as we found seats together for the next session.

"That's her daughter," our mutual friend shouted above the rising din. "But that's only part of the story. I wanted you two to meet because you're both actresses. Kate played Anna in the national Broadway tour of *The King and I*." As though that wasn't impressive enough she added, "with Yul Brynner." And my jaw dropped. I will not lie; I was duly star-struck: not only was Francesca Battistelli Kate's daughter but she herself had whistled a happy tune on Broadway and danced with The King.

We sat close and leaned into one another to share details just as the speaker took the platform. When the hour was past, we moved out against the incoming throng and got separated. It wasn't until the next day that I found her again, which had given me ample time to formulate a plethora of questions for the regal blond with wisdom to share.

"I'd love to hear a bit of your story," I invited over lunch.

Kate graciously launched into an abridged version of the past thirty years of her life. While she had originally been cast as the understudy to the female lead, somewhere around Buffalo the woman playing the English tutor fell ill. For two entire weeks Kate took over the role. By the end of her stint, Yul Brynner was emphatic that she remain his leading lady, and the rest, as they say, is history. Only . . . not entirely, for that is where her story truly began.

On tour, Kate met her husband over the footlights. He was the Associate Conductor and she the Leading Lady. "Looking back I see that God put us together to raise Franny," Kate told me intimately. "A performer and a composer for parents. The only thing missing was faith. Neither of us were Christians when we got married. But shortly after, we met a woman who kept inviting us to church. She was adamant we come. 'They have the best choir you've ever heard,' she told us. Eventually we ran out of excuses and went with her one Sunday morning. It was the last stop on the F train in Queens, New York, and we were the only white people in the all-black congregation. And there was no way we were leaving there that morning anything other than saved."

"We got married in '83, became Christians in '84, and had Franny in '85." Our salad plates were cleared away and the main course set down. "I was a baby Christian during her baby years."

It was during those years that Kate and her husband felt God lead them out of New York and away from their musical theater life. Looking back now Kate recognizes that she'd hit her ceiling as a performer. She had learned and done all that God had for her there in NYC and the world of Broadway. However, over the next two decades, as she grew in faith and raised her talented only child, Kate watched as the Lord made apparent His plans for their musical family.

While I had been curious about Kate's life, given our shared history as performers, I was suddenly much more curious about what she did to raise a creative daughter who ended up using her talents so fervently for God's glory. So I put it to her plainly over dessert. "I have a son who wants nothing more than to become a worship leader. He's only twelve, but already able to learn just about anything on the guitar. What advice do you have for me, as his mother?"

"Immerse him." Those two words came out fast and strong, and she finished telling her story with this: "I'd gone as far as I was going to go, as high as I was going to fly in my career as a performer. However, when Franny wanted to sing and play and dance—whatever she wanted to do—I gave her every opportunity, and my ceiling became her starting point. Everything that I knew and shared became her platform. And God has blown the roof off every dream we'd ever had for ourselves because she began from a place of faith, giving every creative thing she had right back to Him."

Kate told me to immerse my musically gifted son in the arts, let him learn from the best local teachers, get him into voice lessons too, take him to concerts, and introduce him to as many instruments as he wants. "Of course this costs money, lots of it! When Franny was young I worked an extra job, selling perfume in high-end department stores. It was hard on the feet, but it paid for her guitar. It's the same guitar she uses onstage today." And then she told me not only to immerse him in music but to immerse him in the Holy Spirit. "I do not believe that there's a Jr. Holy Spirit for our children. When they put their faith in Christ, they get every bit of Him up front. So immerse him in the study of God's Word, immerse him in youth group gatherings, and immerse him in serving at church with all his gifts."

When I came home from my trip I shared Kate's advice with my husband, and he nodded, because God had already been speaking the same lesson to his heart. "Why don't I offer to lead worship with him for the sixth-grade Sunday school class next fall? That way he doesn't just learn all of the songs; I can disciple him along the way—teach him what it means to lead others in worship."

Immerse him.

Let me encourage you to do the same with your little ones. Immerse your children in the overflow of *your* own creative interests, then discover what unique talents *they* possess and immerse them in their individual interests as well. Surround them with examples of what other children are doing around the world with the special gifts they've been given—the breadth and width of other inspired kids.

> Immerse your children in the overflow of *your* own creative interests, then discover what unique talents *they* possess and immerse them in their individual interests as well.

This generation of young people is growing up in a digital age with examples jamming up their Instagram feed and flooding their YouTube channels. Invitation and opportunity to join in their own Renaissance Faire is right at their little fingertips. When the time is right, you can immerse them here as well. They are going to learn their way around social media eventually; why not show them from the start what a powerful resource it can be for kingdom work? Show them what you're doing, all that you're learning, and the boundaries you set for yourself. Let them see what it looks like to build a healthy online platform.

Immerse them. This is the refrain of our Renaissance song, sung over and over again to our own hearts, and now also into the lives of our precious people. They too need lifeguards, and we have the awesome privilege of not only immersing them in the living water of faith and family, but we get to be their first flesh-and-blood floatation devices out into the creative world via this digital age.

Sitting in the car-pool lane at my children's school, I scrolled through Instagram. When I came across the magazine-worthy picture of a young ballerina midair, I stopped. Tapping the heart on my iPhone screen didn't seem like strong enough affirmation. I wanted the child's mother to hear me say, "I cannot fathom the number of hours you've spent watching your girl practice pirouettes over the past decade. This is breathtaking." Though I never danced like this child, I knew instinctively that her form was perfect. From the pointed toes to the elegant tilt of her chin. Barely a day over twelve, this young woman was exceptionally gifted.

Looking down beneath the picture I read her mother's caption: "Anna dancing pointe to the classic hymn 'How Great Thou Art,' at the Tennessee Performing Arts Center." This gifted young girl had given her talent up as an act of worship in front of hundreds of secular audience members. Within the feed of comments, I tagged another friend on Instagram. Wynter was also a mother who needed to see this beautiful picture of young talent. In this digital age, it's easy to connect like-minded people online by simply typing their name into a thread on social media and, *voilà*, new friends are made. With just a few strokes of my thumb across a cell phone screen, I introduced two mothers.

Wynter Evans Pitts is the author of *For Girls Like You*, a devotional for little women ages 7 to 10, and the founder and editor behind the quarterly magazine by the same name. Along with her daily offering of motherhood, God is using Wynter's talent as a writer and a woman of deep faith, braiding them together into one encouraging work of art after another.

In each quarterly issue, Wynter highlights the stories of young ladies from all corners of the globe who are doing extraordinary things with their unique passions and abilities. From singers and sports stars to young entrepreneurs, girls are inspiring one another to discover their own delightful God-design. That's why I shared the picture of the young ballerina on Instagram with Wynter that day. She's always on the lookout for young women who are using their gifts as a platform to testify about who God is and how much He loves them.

Like Kate and Francesca Battistelli, Wynter and her girls are another beautiful example of a mother's ceiling becoming a child's foundation. Last year, Wynter's oldest daughter became one of the featured stories in *For Girls Like You*. Alena is the young actress who played Danielle

Jordan in the Kendrick Brothers film *War Room*, a major motion picture starring Priscilla Shirer and T. C. Stallings.

As Alena prepared for her audition, Wynter and her husband used the exciting opportunity to teach their child that everything God chooses to do in our lives is for *His* glory and *our* good. If Alena was cast, God was sovereign and good; but if she didn't get the part, He was still good, there on His throne, working it all together for *His* glory and *her* good. They spoke these words of truth over their daughter, and played the worship song "For My Good" again and again. During the anxious days of waiting to see if Alena would be cast in the much-hoped-for role, they played this song on a constant loop, immersing her in the promise that God was not only good but had a specific plan for her life.

> What a privilege we have not only to pursue this creative life of faith for ourselves, but also to pass the Renaissance baton to our children. Partnering with them, baptizing them in the overflow of an inspired home life.

And when she was given the role and began filming, Alena was immersed on-set with some of the biggest names in Christian filmmaking. Each morning before the first scene of the day was shot, they sat together for devotions and prayer.

> If I have seen further, it is by standing on the shoulders of giants.
>
> Isaac Newton, 1676

At a young age, Alena learned that God gives us various gifts for His glory. Sometimes we're privileged to use them in exciting ways in front of the masses, but other times they're simply those things that we enjoy privately. And a young talented girl got to learn these things from her mother first. What a privilege we have not only to pursue this creative life of faith for ourselves, but also to pass the Renaissance baton to our children. Partnering with them, baptizing them in the overflow of an inspired home life.

Cultivating Genius

There is a quiet hour that descends upon our home a few times every week, like the holy cloud over the Old Testament tabernacle. God's presence comes to dwell among His people as silence sinks into the sturdy frame of our house, into the bones of each family member. Within the protective casing of these sacred sixty minutes, books and sketchpads, watercolors and charcoal come out. Dreams are dreamed and visions cast, and children pick up instruments, try their hands at comic book illustration, begin a story, and borrow my camera to explore their world through a lens. We call it our Genius Hour—similar to a mother's sanctified creative time, only this time is allotted for every member of the family.

Google was one of the first to initiate this idea of a genius hour in their corporation. Employees are encouraged to spend up to 20 percent of their workdays on whatever fires them up. The philosophy is simple: when people explore what interests them, they're most productive. It's not surprising that 50 percent of Google's newest projects are born in those genius moments.

I wonder what genius might be lurking in the dream-lives of your children? What untapped passion might they find if you bring them into those sanctified creative moments? What if we, like Google, allowed our young people to explore what fires them up? I've recently heard various studies predicting that over half of the jobs our children's generation will occupy have yet to be invented. Mind blowing!

Who better to conceive and invent these new careers, technologies, services, and products than our own inspired sons and daughters, in the safe, quiet space of our home lives? Join them as they imagine the possibilities. Cheer them on as they learn to film and edit Claymation or Lego movies at the kitchen table with your iPhone. As dinner simmers on the stove behind them, so much good is simmering in their minds too—marinating and bubbling up into an absolute feast. Taste and see what God has planned for them. Watch them go! Let's learn from one another in this meeting place where two Renaissance generations converge under one sweeping canopy called home.

> The next generation is watching us moms—always watching, seeing what we make, how we make it, and who we make it for.

The next generation is watching us moms—always watching, seeing what we make, how we make it, and who we make it for. They follow our example out into their own inspired faith lives. Turning to us for approval. "Atta girl . . . Atta boy!" At our side they discover what it means to have both roots and wings. Dreaming big dreams then trying their hands at everything that inspires them, all while grounded in the safe soil of family. What a gift we give to them. And miracle of miracles, wouldn't you know, they give right back—teaching us how to jump in unhindered. Believing that cardboard and silver spray paint can transform a boy into a robot; that scotch tape and feathers are all you need to fly.

Chapter Fifteen

Doxology

The arts and the sciences do have a place in the Christian life—they are not peripheral. For a Christian, redeemed by the work of Christ and living within the norms of Scripture and under the leadership of the Holy Spirit, the Lordship of Christ should include an interest in the arts. A Christian should use these arts to the glory of God, not just as tracts, mind you, but as things of beauty to the praise of God. An art work can be a doxology in itself.

Francis A. Schaeffer

At the end of each service, we stood together as a whole, the church worshipping as one voice through the hallowed tones of the doxology. This was our congregational affirmation in the church of my youth, sung with thanksgiving. It was tradition, yes, but also a tangible and vocal commitment of faith. And so it was when I married my husband that I couldn't imagine any better way to conclude our vows except with the doxology. Well, that and a kiss, of course. So we did both. We kissed and they cheered, then everyone stood and sang:

Praise God from whom all blessings flow;
Praise Him all creatures here below;
Praise Him above, ye heavenly host;
Praise Father, Son, and Holy Ghost. Amen.

Thomas Ken, 1674

That's what we're doing now, here at the end of this journey together. We're linking arms with one another across the aisles and miles, singing it loud, because we serve a great, gift-giving God. The One who fashioned each intricate piece of you, both the glory gold and earthen clay parts, has amazing things in store. It's a treasure hunt you're now on, following the clues along the path laid specifically for your life. And each clue is wrapped in marvelously made you, in your children and the life you share, and in the inspiration that fills your sails. Though the vision may be long in coming, have courage!

> This season is sacred, but there is sacred beyond this season.

His master said to him, "Well done, good and faithful slave. You were faithful with a few things, I will put you in charge of many things; enter into the joy of your master." (Matt. 25:23)

Be faithful in the little things, in the little moments, with the little people there in your holy Jerusalem, amidst sanctified mothering days. Be faithful to the family you have been given, the talents entrusted to you alone, and the vision projected into the recesses of your heart. This season is sacred, but there is sacred beyond this season. And when the time is right for you to share your gifts with the world, venture out in confidence and testify with boldness and beauty.

Whatever you do in word or deed [or artistry], do all in the name of the Lord Jesus, giving thanks through Him to God the Father. (Col. 3:17)

This is our doxology, our send-off drenched in praise to the One who masterfully made you. We affirm your delightful uniqueness, as we did at the start, and acknowledge that being a creative woman in this season of life is marvelous, albeit not easy. *Press on.*

Life is a buffet, and every creative brings her own dish to offer at the banqueting table. Some need to be fed by your unique words, refreshed by the living water dripping from your creative images, and sung into deeper faith through the strains of your cello song. And if you don't paint it, write it, sing it, bake it, sew it, say it . . . they may go hungry. *So press on.*

Pick up your brush and offer up your own brand of color to the world. We value your contribution at this Renaissance Faire, and believe in your ability to impact this world through your life creative. You, dear mom, are making a difference. You're doing it right there in your home, feeding the needs of the world through uniquely created you. *Press on.*

Your life, exactly as God has blessed it, was created for the illuminating purpose of being His light in the fullness of all the challenges, the triumphs, the weary moments, and the glory-filled joys through which you daily walk. Though you may not have hours each day to focus on your craft, make no mistake that your widow's mite is a thing of beauty to God. Coupled with God's supernatural potential, your art has the power to bring about a great harvest. Though at times it may seem slow and small, *press on.* You're doing the right thing.

> Your widow's mite is a thing of beauty to God. Coupled with God's supernatural potential, your art has the power to bring about a great harvest.

In a world that celebrates big wins and great finishes, it can be hard to embrace slow starts and small endings.

Emily P. Freeman

We See You

Dear friends, we are passionate about how God made you. Fearfully. Wonderfully. Intentionally. Creatively. And we don't want you to doubt for one moment His joy over your design, or the gospel power bound up in your creative heart. We don't want you to question His delight in your unique dreams as you balance so many things, every facet for His glory. He is near, enjoying the glory-crash of your creative life in Him. Of course, this doesn't mean the road will be easy.

Is it possible that your dreams may end up looking different from what you penned in your journal? Could it be that God's guiding Spirit will take you down some varied path? Are you open to accepting that God prepared many small good works for you, rather than one big one, like a splattering of faithful blog posts rather than a book bound up with a cover and a spine? And could it be that He's not finished with you yet? Absolutely. Time and again, yes! So don't you stop! You keep pressing in to Him and pressing on where His faithful Holy Spirit directs.

As you arrange the table full of freshly baked food, preparing to welcome neighbors into your midst, remember that your meal is important. Your gift in the kitchen feeds more than stomachs—you are sharing the gospel message of love through hospitality.

When you design a beautiful website, you draw the eye of the reader into a new space, visually capturing them. In that space a woman gifted with words can bring joy, encouragement, and hope to all who enter. Both gifts are important—yours and hers.

That song you pen late at night when the melodies captivate your weary soul will speak to the masses. Or maybe it will only speak to your family as you play and sing by the fire pit as little ones roast marshmallows. Whether heard by hundreds, or by three, your gift is important.

We see you as you decorate your home. We see your photos online, and we feel the power of your particular art when a perfectly coordinated room creates peace. Don't assume your art unworthy; it is indeed a grand offering to your loved ones and the world. Your gift of design was perfectly designed. We recognize this, and we thank you for revealing the beauty of life right there in your Instagram feed.

This book is our cry of praise—our acknowledgment of your creative presence in this glorious, artistic Renaissance. And here at the end we've got a word for you: *Press in and press on, dear friends!* Boldly live your unique design right there where you are, there in the midst of motherhood.

Write it out, sing it loud, say it in the syncopated rhythm of a spoken-word poem, paint it, create it, lay it down, and live it out in a one woman show at your next women's ministry event. Press on in the little moments of your mothering, married, ministry-loving days. And in this way, follow the call to be authentically true to who you are each and every moment.

His creative.

> Then I heard the voice of the Lord, saying, "Whom shall I send, and who will go for Us?" Then I said, "Here am I. Send me!" (Isa. 6:8)

This is our doxology. May we respond collectively, and individually, today: "Here am I. Send me. Send consecrated, creative me."

NOTES

The number preceding each note below is the page number on which the related text appears.

Introduction

11. *Carter:* Hodding Carter Jr., *Where Main Street Meets the River* (New York: Rinehart, 1953), 337.
13. *Bonhoeffer:* Dietrich Bonhoeffer, *Life Together* (New York: Harper-Collins, 1954), 57.

Chapter 1: A New Renaissance

15. *Augustine:* Augustine, *The Confessions*, Oxford World's Classics (New York: Oxford Paperbacks, 2009), book 10, chapter 8 (15), p. 187.
23. *Hanson:* Erin Hanson, *The Poetic Underground*, thepoeticunder ground.com (2014), reprinted by permission.

Chapter 2: Confined Yet Unhindered

29. *McManus:* Erwin Raphael McManus, "The Artisan: A Manifesto of Human Creativity—Erwin Raphael McManus," Hillsong guest blog, July 7, 2015, http://hillsong.com/collected/blog/2015/07/the -artisan-a-manifesto-of-human-creativity-erwin-raphael-mcmanus/.
30. *Clarkson:* You can connect with Sally at SallyClarkson.com.

Chapter 3: Beyond Jerusalem

39. *Potter:* Quoted in Margaret Mackey, ed., *Beatrix Potter's Peter Rabbit: A Children's Classic at 100* (Lanham, MD: Scarecrow Press, 2002), 43.

40. *Modersohn-Becker:* Paula Modersohn-Becker, *The Letters and Journals*, ed. and trans. Arthur S. Wensinger and Carole Clew Hoey (Evanston, IL: Northwestern University Press, 1998), 123.

Chapter 4: Renaissance Faire

51. *Cooper:* Sean Cooper, *People Who Sing Jesus* (Longwood, FL: True North Foundation, 2011), 17.
61. *Camealy:* Kris Camealy, "Stretch," blog, May 28, 2015, http://kriscamealy.com/stretch-2/.

Chapter 5: Our Most Beautiful Creations

63. *Wierenga:* Emily T. Wierenga, *Atlas Girl* (Grand Rapids: Baker, 2014), 244.
69. *Morison:* Written on the plaque beside Samuel Eliot Morison's statue on the Commonwealth Mall in Boston, Massachusetts.
71. *Rogers:* Mindy Rogers, 2014, quoted by Wendy Speake, "Writing, Motherhood, and Sacrifice," blog, September 14, 2015, http://wendyspeake.com/writing-motherhood-sacrifice/. Used by permission.
72. *Woolf:* Virginia Woolf, *A Writer's Diary* (New York: Harcourt Brace, 1954), 13.

Chapter 6: Making Space

75. *Tankersley:* Leeana Tankersley, "Less Trying, More Trusting," blog, March 16, 2015, http://www.leeanatankersley.com/2015/03/less-trying-trusting/.
82. *Bush:* Barbara Bush, address to Republican National Committee (Houston, TX, August 19, 1992), transcribed on Speech Vault, accessed November 18, 2015, www.speeches-usa.com/Transcripts/barbara_bush-1992rnc.html.

Chapter 7: Renaissance Worship

87. *Voskamp:* Ann Voskamp, "A Bit of Instructions on How to Live a Good Life: How to Be an Artist, a Parent, a Creative, a Dreamer," blog, June 23, 2014, http://www.aholyexperience.com/2014/06/a

-bit-of-instructions-on-how-to-live-a-good-life-how-to-be-an-artist
-a-parent-a-creative-a-dreamer/.
95–96. *Lewis:* C. S. Lewis, *The Screwtape Letters* (New York: Harper-
One, 1942), 71.

Chapter 8: The Art of Home
99. *Austen:* Jane Austen, *Emma* (Chenango Forks, NY: Wild Joy Press,
2009), 168.
108. *Michaels:* Melissa Michaels, *Love the Home You Have* (Eugene,
OR: Harvest House, 2015), 70.
109–10. *Manning:* Brennan Manning, *The Ragamuffin Gospel: Good
News for the Bedraggled, Beat-Up and Burnt Out* (Colorado Springs:
Multnomah, 2005), 59–60.
110. *Smith:* This is Myquillyn Smith's *Nesting Place* blog tagline, http://
www.thenester.com/.

Chapter 9: The Pull of the Tide
113. *Clarkson:* Sally Clarkson, "The Secret to Making It to the End
of December Without Blowing Apart," blog, December 16, 2012,
http://sallyclarkson.com/the-secret-to-making-it-to-the-end-of
-december-without-blowing-apart/.
118. *Milne:* Alan Alexander Milne, *The Complete Tales of Winnie the
Pooh* (New York: Penguin, 1992), 120.

Chapter 10: When God Calls a Mother
127. *Lucado:* Max Lucado, *The Applause of Heaven* (Nashville: Thomas
Nelson, 1990), 154.

Chapter 11: A Business of Art in the Busyness of Motherhood
141. *Gaines:* "The Gathering Testimony: Joanna Gaines," 1:10, You-
Tube video, posted by Baylor University, April 1, 2015, https://
www.youtube.com/watch?v=t7iPEDnqwm0.

Chapter 12: Renaissance Mom in a Digital Age

155. *Caine:* Christine Caine, Instagram, https://www.instagram.com
/p/52ROy9THGQ/?taken-by=christinecaine.

Chapter 13: When Art Turns a Profit

167. *Hyatt:* Michael Hyatt, "Three Reasons You Shoundn't Be Bashful About Selling Your Own Products," blog, November 10, 2014, http://michaelhyatt.com/bashful-about-selling.html.
172. *McManus:* Erwin Raphael McManus, *The Artisan Soul: Crafting Your Life into a Work of Art* (New York: HarperOne), 143.
177. *Thoreau:* Henry David Thoreau, *Walden and Other Writings*, ed. Brooks Atkinson (New York: Random House, 2000), 303.

Chapter 14: Renaissance Rising

181. *Battistelli:* Kate Battistelli, *Growing Great Kids* (Lake Mary, FL: Charisma House, 2012), 6.
182. *Goff:* Bob Goff, *Love Does* (Nashville: Nelson Books, 2012), 2.
190. *Newton:* Isaac Newton, *The Correspondence of Isaac Newton: 1661–1675*, ed. H. W. Turnbull (London: Cambridge University Press, 1959), 416.

Chapter 15: Doxology

193. *Schaeffer:* Francis A. Schaeffer, *Art and the Bible* (Downers Grove, IL: InterVarsity Press, 1973), 10.
195. *Freeman:* Emily P. Freeman, Instagram, https://www.instagram.com/p/4xrZURnRez/?taken-by=emilypfreeman. Used by permission.

ACKNOWLEDGMENTS

To our agent, *Ruth Samsel*, who caught the vision of this holy Renaissance in the lobby of a conference center! We are humbled beyond belief that you would take under your wing two moms who knew so little about the book-publishing process. It's been a joy-filled education.

Likewise, *Kregel Publications*—you believed in the gospel message at the heart of this book from the very beginning and worked with us to refine it. We are grateful to the Lord for each one of you.

To *Alle McCloskey and Lindsey Hartz*, who joined forces with us in this life creative. We are so thankful for the vision you bring and the encouragement you rain down on us. Thank you for walking this path with us.

To our Creative Retreat gals, *Angie, Bethany, Jenni, and Tammy*—you were the flesh-and-blood start to all of this. We looked at what we had with you and asked the Lord how we might bottle it up and share it with others. This book is His answer.

from Wendy . . .
To my husband, Matt—Thank you for lifting me back up each time I lay it all down for you and the boys. You are the most tangible expression of God's love to me. *Caleb, Brody, and Asher*—You three have taught me more about the glorious creativity of God than anyone else. Each one of you is fearfully and wonderfully made, and I have no doubt that your individual God-designs will bring glory and honor and fame to Jesus. Dear *Mom*—From the time I belted out songs on the fireplace hearth until today, you have been my biggest fan. Thank you for taking the boys for long weekends at Grandma's house, giving me the space to write many of these pages. *Dad and Anita*—No one else has supported

me as an artist more than you two! Paying for classes and flying to shows, always celebrating every success. Thank you! *Amber Rogers and Christy Nueman*—You prayed me through this process. Any fruit that comes from this book is yours as much as mine. And *Kelli Stuart*—I cannot put into words the gratitude I feel that God would give me you! You are my lifeguard! And I am a better writer and a clearer reflection of our Savior because of you.

from Kelli . . .

To my husband, Lee—You've been my cheerleader since I was just a kid with a dream. If it weren't for you pushing me outside my comfort zone I never would have stepped onto this Renaissance path. Thank you for believing in me before I believed in myself. *Sloan, Katya, Landon, and Annika*—You inspire me every day with your creativity, your joy, your enthusiasm for life, and your imagination. I could not be more thankful that God saw fit to make me your mom. *Mom and Dad*—You always made me believe that anything was possible with just a little bit of courage and a lot of hard work. Thanks for teaching me what it means to be brave and to live life to the fullest. *Herb and Barbara*—You shared the gift of your son with me, then loved me like a daughter. Herb, I miss you every day and though I long to have you back, I would never ask that of you. Barbara, thanks for modeling what it means to love your husband fully both in life and in death. To the many dear friends who loved me and supported me and cheered me on through this process—thank you. I couldn't have done it without you. And *Wendy*—God knew I needed a sister, and I couldn't be more grateful that He sent me you so many years ago. What a privilege to journey through this life with you, my dear friend.

ABOUT THE AUTHORS

Wendy Speake is a trained actress and passionate Bible teacher who ministers to women's hearts through storytelling and biblical life applications. During her career in Hollywood, on shows such as *JAG*, *Melrose Place*, *Star Trek: Voyager*, and *Roswell*, Wendy found herself longing to tell stories that edify and encourage women. Today she does just that, using dramatic monologues, comedy, poetry, and the study of God's Word to move audiences closer to Jesus.

Wendy coauthored the book *Triggers: Exchanging Parents' Angry Reactions for Gentle Biblical Responses* with Amber Lia (2016, BRU Press). She speaks extensively throughout the United States and is a regular contributor to The MOB Society and Great Homeschool Conventions. Wendy and her husband, Matt, have been married fifteen years and reside in Southern California with their three ruddy boys. You can connect with Wendy at WendySpeake.com.

Kelli Stuart is a writer and a storyteller at heart. A graduate of Baylor University with a degree in English professional writing and a minor in Russian, Kelli is a well-known blogger and speaker who has traveled extensively, constantly honing her craft of weaving words into tales as she experiences life and the world. Kelli has written for and represented such brands as *The Huffington Post*, 5 Minutes for Mom, Compassion International, Extraordinary Mommy,

The MOB Society, and Short Fiction Break. Kelli's first novel, *Like a River from Its Course*, released earlier in 2016 to rave reviews. She also coauthored the book *Dare 2B Wise: 10 Minute Devotions 2 Inspire Courageous Living* with Joe White. Kelli is a wife, a homeschooling mom, and the driver of a (smokin' hot) minivan. She lives in Tampa, Florida, with her husband and four children. You can find out more about Kelli at KelliStuart.com.